How to Get the Most from God's Word

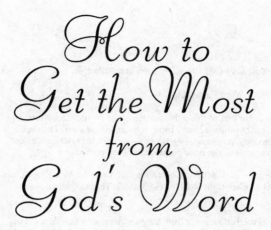

How to Get the Most from God's Word

JOHN MACARTHUR, JR.

WORD PUBLISHING
Dallas • London • Vancouver • Melbourne

How to Get the Most from God's Word by John MacArthur, Jr.

Library of Congress Cataloging-in-Publication Data

MacArthur, John, 1939–
How to get the most from God's word / John MacArthur, Jr.
p. cm.
Includes index.
ISBN 0-8499- 4093-1
1. Bible—Introductions. 2. Bible—Reading. I. Title.
BS475.2.M33 1997
220.1—dc21 97-27916
CIP

Printed in the United States of America.

05 04 03 02 01 00 99 98 97
10 9 8 7 6 5 4 3 2

Table of Contents

Part Three

KNOW HOW TO STUDY THE BIBLE

Foreword

From the day I sensed the call of God into full-time ministry, the driving passion of my life has been simply to understand God's Word and then to make it understandable to others. All my pastoral energies—in my preaching, shepherding, teaching, writing, and even visitation—are focused on that one goal. Every aspect of my work is simply a means to that end.

I have never aspired to be known as either an academic theologian or a distinguished clergyman. I simply want to know what the Word of God means and to make it known to others. That insatiable craving is what has motivated me from the beginning of my ministry.

Although I have often dealt with theological questions and doctrinal controversies in my writing and preaching, I have never done so from a merely academic or polemic perspective. I certainly have never done so out of a love of debate. Again, the only compelling factor for me has been a burning desire to understand God's Word accurately and teach it with precision.

When it comes to discerning the truth of God, popular opinion, conventional wisdom, and the latest "scholarship" of cynics are of no concern to me whatsoever. Even the question of whether some point of doctrine fits with this or that historic tradition matters little to me. I simply want to understand what the Bible means by what it says.

It is my conviction that the Bible is not difficult for the believing heart to understand. And the more I understand, the more unshakable is my conviction that the Bible is the living, authoritative, inerrant Word of God. It has this remarkable effect on me: the more

I study it, the more I hunger to know. So God's Word is not only the thing that satisfies my appetite, but it also arouses an even deeper hunger for more.

Sharing that hunger with others has always been the supreme joy of my heart as a pastor. To that end, I have devoted the past two years of my life to the production of a new study Bible. The project has been the greatest undertaking of my life, and one of the most profitable tasks I have ever embarked upon.

In conjunction with the release of this study Bible, I have assembled the volume you now hold in your hands. The material represented here spans thirty years of my writing and preaching ministry. These chapters comprise the heart of what I have taught about God's Word, how to study it, and how to discern its meaning for yourself. Some of these chapters have been published in various formats, but they are brought together here for the first time in a new volume.

My prayer is that this book will be helpful to you as you seek to feed your own appetite for knowing and understanding the Word of God.

John MacArthur, Jr.

Chapter One
How Can We Know God?

All mankind is trapped on planet Earth, captive to time and space and surrounded by an endless universe. Many sense in the deepest parts of their beings that there is an ultimate power or God. And so they try to discover how they can know this Supreme Being. The result is religion, the invention of man in his attempt to find God.

Christianity, however, teaches that we don't find God, because God has already found us. He has disclosed Himself to us through His Word. In the Old and New Testaments of Holy Scripture we have the unveiling of God.

The Bible bridges the entire history of the earth. During those long centuries God was always disclosing Himself, because it is in His nature to communicate. An artist paints and a singer sings because the ability is in them. God speaks because He desires to make Himself known to His creatures.

Francis Schaeffer, referring to God, wrote, "He is there, and He is not silent."

In the beginning God spoke and the universe was born out of nothing. We read how He spoke to Adam, to Abraham, to Moses, and to the prophets. The Jews understood God as a speaking God, and through His messengers they often heard the expression "Thus says the Lord." In the books of the Prophets we read it often. "Therefore, say to them, 'Thus says the LORD of hosts: "Return to Me," says the LORD of hosts, "and I will return to you," says the LORD of hosts' " (Zech. 1:3). Throughout the Book of Ezekiel we read, "And He said to me," when God spoke to Ezekiel and called him "Son of man" ninety-one times (Ezek. 2:1; 3:3, 4, 10).

When Jesus came into the world, He was called the Word. It was an appropriate name for God's revelation in the flesh—the living Word. "In the beginning was the Word, and the Word was with God, and the Word was God. . . . And the Word became flesh and dwelt among us, and we beheld His glory, the glory as of the only begotten of the Father, full of grace and truth" (John 1:1, 14).

What God has spoken does not change. "Forever, O Lord, Your word is settled in heaven" (Ps. 119:89). Jesus said, "Heaven and earth will pass away, but My words will by no means pass away" (Matt. 24:35). And Peter wrote, "But the word of the Lord endures forever" (1 Pet. 1:25).

When God Is Silent

The God who speaks, however, sometimes chooses to remain silent for a time. And when He does, it is in judgment. For example, God freely communicated with King Saul, but Saul's repeated rejection of the Lord and his frequent disobedience finally caught up with him. When Saul called on the Lord, he received no answer. "The Lord did not answer him, either by dreams or by Urim or by the prophets" (1 Sam. 28:6).

There came a time when God's patience with Israel was exhausted. He told Jeremiah, the weeping prophet, "Do not pray for this people . . . I will not hear their cry" (Jer. 14:11, 12).

We read in the Book of Proverbs that God promised to pour out His Spirit and to make known His words (Prov. 1:23). But what happens to those who refuse to listen? We are not left to guess.

> Because I have called and you refused; I have stretched out my hand and no one regarded; Because you disdained all my counsel; and would have none of my rebuke; I also will laugh at your calamity; I will mock when your terror comes; When your terror comes like a storm; and your destruction comes like a whirlwind; when distress and anguish

> come upon you. "Then they will call on me, but I will not answer; They will seek me diligently, but they will not find me." (Prov. 1:24–28)

God freely shares Himself, but if we reject Him—that's it.

God Is Personal

What is God like—this Revealer who speaks? First, the God who speaks is personal. He calls Himself *I* and addresses those to whom He speaks as *you.* Moses asked God what His name was. "And God said to Moses, 'I AM WHO I AM.' And He said, 'Thus you shall say to the children of Israel, 'I AM has sent me to you' "(Ex. 3:14).

I AM indicates personality. God Himself had a name, even as He gave names to others—to Abraham and to Israel. The name *I AM* stands for a free, purposeful, self-sufficient personality. God is what He wants to be, and He tells us that by His choice of a name.

God is not a floating fog, not an *it.* He is not an aimless, blind force. He is not cosmic energy. God is an almighty, self-existing, self-determining being with mind and will. He is a person!

If you read through the Bible, you find that God is not only personal, but that He is tripersonal. In the opening words of Genesis God said, "Then God said, 'Let Us make man in *Our* image, according to *Our* likeness' " (Gen. 1:26, author's italics). In the Psalms, we have a record of God speaking to God: "The *Lord* said to my Lord" (Ps. 110:1, author's italics). The New Testament name for God is Father, Son, and Holy Spirit (Matt. 28:19). God is personal.

A second characteristic of the Revealer God is that He is moral. He is the Holy One who is supremely concerned about right and wrong. Morality is a top priority with God. This is wonderfully expressed in His words to Moses: "The Lord God, merciful and gracious, longsuffering, and abounding in goodness and truth, keeping mercy for thousands, forgiving iniquity and transgression and sin, by no means clearing the guilty" (Ex. 34:6, 7).

This may seem contradictory. After speaking of His grace, mercy, and forgiveness, God says that He won't let the guilty go unpunished. This assures us that God is *just,* and that He will not merely say to guilty people, "It's all right. I'll let you off the hook." God does show mercy, but someone has to pay the penalty for sin. The Gospels make it clear that the "Someone" is Jesus Christ.

Getting to Know the Unknown God

A third aspect of the nature of God is that He not only is personal and moral, but He is also the beginning, the maintainer, and the end of all creation. We read in Romans that "Of Him and through Him and to Him are all things" (11:36).

Listen over the shoulder of Paul as he addressed the Athenians on Mars Hill. In effect he said, "Men, as I was coming into your city, I noted all the religious statues you have. Obviously, you're a religious bunch. I even found one statue dedicated to the 'unknown god.' Well, I would like you to meet Him. I know Him very well" (Acts 17:23, author's paraphrase).

Paul told his listeners that God was the source of everything: "God, who made the world and everything in it, since He is Lord of heaven and earth, does not dwell in temples made with hands"(Acts 17:24). God also sustains everything: "He gives to all life, breath, and all things. . . . for in Him we live and move and have our being, as also some of your own poets have said, 'For we are also His offspring.' " (vv. 25, 28). And God is the end, the goal, the purpose of all: "So that they should seek the Lord, in the hope that they might grope for Him and find Him" (v. 27).

Man's destiny is to seek and to know this God who gives and sustains life. The whole purpose of man's existence is fulfilled only when he knows God; and man's search for God must begin and end in the Scriptures because that is where God has revealed Himself. A personal resource, such as the *MacArthur Study Bible,* can help you learn more about God and what His plan is for your life.

God Is Available

All this is impressive, but it would not mean much if the One who speaks was not available to us. He is available—that is the whole purpose of His self-revelation. He *wants* us to know Him. Because God is a person, He wants to have fellowship with us. The fact He is moral indicates He wants to deal with us righteously. The fact He is the source, the sustainer, and the end of all creation means our destinies are dependent on our relationship to Him. The fact He is available to us is an exciting concept. We can come into a full relationship with the God who speaks—but only through the way that is made so clear to us in His revelation, the Bible. Jesus said, "I am the way, the truth, and the life. No one comes to the Father except through Me" (John 14:6). Peter declared, "Nor is there salvation in any other, for there is no other name under heaven given among men by which we must be saved" (Acts 4:12).

Chapter Two
How Has God Spoken to Us?

The God who speaks has done so in the Bible—His revelation to us. It is important we understand this, because much "new revelation" is being claimed today.[1]

After I had spoken at a seminar, a young woman came to me and asked, "You don't believe there is any more revelation being given today, do you?"

"No," I replied, "I believe the revelation of God is completed."

"Well, I happen to go to a church where we have an apostle," she insisted.

"That's very interesting. Who is he—Peter, James, John, or Paul?"

"Oh, he's not any of those, but he is an apostle."

"How do you know he is an apostle?"

"Because he speaks direct revelation from God."

I blinked. "You mean, when he gets up and talks, it isn't just a sermon, but it's God speaking through him?"

"That's right. He gives direct revelations every Sunday."

How can we evaluate a claim such as that? What shall we think when we go to a Christian bookstore and pick up a book that describes a revealed vision from God and contradicts or adds to the Bible?

For the answer, we must look to the origin of the claimed message. Is it certain that it came from God's voluntary act of love in disclosing Himself, or did it actually come from the mind of a person who thought he spoke for God?

Did Moses, having nothing better to do one day, suddenly decide he would record the creation of the world? "Now, let's see. I wonder how this whole world came about. It seems to me that . . ."

That's not how it happened. God told Moses what had occurred, and Moses in obedience, recorded what God revealed to him: "In the beginning God created the heavens and the earth" (Gen. 1:1). This is revelation from God, not a supposition from Moses.

Imagine Isaiah sitting down to write, "Therefore the Lord Himself will give you a sign: Behold, the virgin shall conceive and bear a Son, and shall call His name Immanuel" (Is. 7:14). I couldn't come up with that, but Isaiah did because it was revealed to him.

Envision Micah saying, "You, Bethlehem Ephrathah; though you are little among the thousands of Judah; yet out of you shall come forth to Me; the One to be Ruler in Israel (Mic. 5:2). He couldn't have made this valid prophecy unless it had been revealed to him.

Can you picture David writing in relation to the Crucifixion, "My God, My God, why have You forsaken Me?" (Ps. 22:1) and doing it hundreds of years before Jesus was born, if it had not been revealed to him by God?

The supernatural wisdom and great prophecies in the Bible came from God, not from men. They were God's thoughts and words, not the speculations of men (Matt. 16:17; 2 Pet. 1:21); and nothing is to be added to them (Jude 3; Rev. 22:18, 19). Let's think further about God's revelation.

The World of Nature

God has revealed Himself to us in two ways: through *natural revelation* and through *special revelation.* We can't look at the beauty we see during the day or look at the stars of the night without concluding that Someone greater than us made it all. *Everything* cries of the existence of God and of His work. "For since the creation of the world His invisible attributes are clearly seen, being understood by the things that are made, even His eternal power and Godhead, so that they are without excuse" (Rom. 1:20).

The world of nature reveals three things. The first is God's power. When we look at the created world, we can only stand in awe of the tremendous power that must have been exerted in its formation. For example, one star, Betelgeuse, is twice the size of the earth's orbit around the sun and is 500 light-years away. At 186,000 miles per second, it takes 500 years for its light to reach the Earth. This is only one star on the edge of a universe that contains billions of stars like it. All of this was made by God!

Nature also reveals the Godhead. The Greek word for Godhead stresses God's sovereign deity—the fact that He is God. The God who created the universe is sovereign. He runs the show. He is in complete control.

Third, nature tells us of God's wrath. We read that unbelievers are without excuse when they face God's judgment (Rom. 1:20). It is evident everywhere we look that a curse is on the world—that it is under a moral sentence. The world groans as if in labor, awaiting its redemption (Rom. 8:22).

That briefly is the content of natural revelation.

"Well, it's fuzzy, and hard to understand," you might be tempted to say. But Scripture tells us the fact that God exists is "clearly seen." The revelation from nature is clear. No one can excuse themselves because of ignorance. There is no alibi for the atheist, and there is no excuse for the agnostic.

Results of Rejection

If creation is so clearly the work of a Creator, why have so many missed this conclusion? The difficulty is not in the revelation, but in man.

> Because, although they knew God, they did not glorify Him as God, nor were thankful, but became futile in their thoughts, and their foolish hearts were darkened. . . . They . . . changed the glory of the incorruptible God into an image made like corruptible man—and birds and four-footed animals and creeping things. (Rom. 1:21–23)

When man deliberately rejects the truth that can be known about God through nature, God gives man up to idolatry (v. 23), to sexual impurity (vv. 24–27), and to a reprobate mind (v. 28). As a result man can't know God on his own, even though he lives in a world that shows God's character, attributes, power, and works. Spiritually, man is dead (Eph. 2:1). A dead man doesn't respond. Man is blind (Eph. 4:18). A blind man can't see the truth no matter how well it is illuminated. The same verse tells us that not only is unregenerate man dead and blind, but he is also ignorant. Dead. Blind. Ignorant. His state is the terrible result of sin!

The Light Inside

Natural revelation is not confined to the creation which is external. Natural revelation also comes through our own conscience. This is internal. "What may be known of God is manifest in them" (Rom. 1:19). People today, because of what they have on the inside, are conscious that God exists. Even Albert Einstein felt he had to believe in a cosmic power. He was convinced that a man who did not believe in a cosmic power as the source of all things was a fool.

A person can deny this, of course. "The fool has said in his heart, 'There is no God' " (Ps. 14:1). Interestingly enough, the word *fool* can also be translated "wicked." Atheists are wicked. That is how they get to be atheists. They have wickedly reduced God to nonexistence in order to entertain their sins without a sense of moral obligation.

In order for the fool to say the word *God*, however, he must have a concept of God. And if he has a concept of God, that implies that God is. It is impossible to think of something that is not, therefore, he is trying to eliminate something that his very reasoning powers tell him exists. For the fool to work that hard to deny God's existence is testimony that God must exist, or the fool wouldn't have to worry about getting rid of Him.

Nature, then, is God's disclosure of Himself in man and in man's environment. The astronomer Herschel said, "The broader the field of science grows, the more manifold and irrefutable become the proofs for the eternal existence of a creative and omnipotent wisdom." Linnaeus, the famous professor of medicine and botany from the 1700s, declared, "I have seen the footsteps of God." The astronomer Kepler testified, "In creation I grasped God as if He were in my hands."

A Christian leader of the third century, known for his wisdom, was once asked where he got such wisdom.

> The source of all I have learned is in two books. The one is outwardly small, the other is very large. The former has many pages, the latter only two. The pages of the former are white with many black letters on them. One of the pages of the big book is blue, and the other is green. On the blue page there is one big golden letter and many small silver ones. On the green page there are innumerable colored letters in red, white, yellow, blue, and gold. The small book is the Bible; the large one is nature.

These two "books" belong together. Both testify to the revelation of the one living God; their testimonies are in harmony and point to the power, greatness, and love of the Lord of the world.

Sin Became a Barrier

So we have natural revelation given to us through creation and through our consciences. Natural revelation was fully effective before the Fall of man in the Garden of Eden. Then, there was no sin. There was no barrier. Adam and Eve could live with God out of the depths of pure hearts. God didn't need to write to them in the Garden, but after the Fall natural revelation was not sufficient. Sin placed a barrier between man and Holy God. Someone had to take the punishment for that sin and provide a way to restore man to fellowship with God (2 Cor. 5:21). God foretold through His prophets (in the Old Testament) that such a One would come and later recorded (in the New Testament) how the Son of God came to the world, died, was buried, and then rose from the dead. Jesus Christ became the way.

The New Testament makes this clear. Jesus said, "I am the way, the truth, and the life. No one comes to the Father except through Me" (John 14:6). Peter said, "Nor is there salvation in any other, for there is no other name under heaven given among men by which we must be saved" (Acts 4:12). Jesus told men that they were condemned because they did not believe on Him (John 3:18). Paul declared to the Philippian jailer, "Believe in the Lord Jesus, and you will be saved" (Acts 16:31). Faith in Christ is necessary.

Special Revelation

Special revelation takes up where creation and conscience leave off. Special revelation tells us all we need to know about God—truth that was never before understood. It tells us about God's mercy—about His grace—about how sin can be forgiven. It tells about the sacrifice of Christ—about salvation—about the church.

Special revelation gives us specifics. When God spoke, He didn't mumble. God spoke clearly and to the point. He was precise, even to the choice of words, verb tenses, and distinguishing between plural and singular words.

God's special revelation came progressively. When we read the Book of Genesis, we get part of the revelation of God. It is limited. When we read only the Old Testament, we get only part of the revelation. Scripture is progressive revelation in the sense that it goes from partial to complete—not from error to truth or truth to error.

Some of the Old Testament prophets read what they wrote and tried to figure out exactly what it meant. They searched in their own prophecies to determine who would fulfill the prophecies related to the Messiah and when it would happen (1 Pet. 1:10–12). It was to come later.

Special revelation, then, was a process. First God revealed Himself in a small frame, later in larger measure. First revelation was to a man, then to a family, then to a tribe, then to a nation, then to a race, and ultimately to the world.

God Became Man

How has God revealed Himself in special revelation? He has revealed Himself in three main ways. The first is theophany—the visible appearance of God in some form. We see in the Old Testament that God at times appeared as a man. He and two angels appeared to Abraham as visitors. Abraham greeted the guests and invited them into his house. He asked Sarah to prepare her best culinary delights (Gen. 18:1–8). Imagine Abraham and his wife fixing a meal to entertain God and two angels! In this instance, God assumed human form to appear to Abraham.

There were other ways God revealed Himself in visible form. God appeared to Moses in a burning bush (Ex. 3); He also appeared as the Shekinah Glory in the Tabernacle (Ex. 33–40). Jacob wrestled with a "Man," who was in fact God in human form (Gen. 32:24–32). Theologians call this a Christophany—a pre-incarnate appearance of Christ.

The greatest theophany of all, in a sense, is the coming of the Lord Jesus Christ in human form to walk on earth and to dwell with men. God is not a man, as the Bible clearly teaches. "God is Spirit" (John 4:24), but He has chosen to reveal Himself in human form, and most perfectly in Jesus Christ.

Note that in each of these cases, God's special revelation accomplished a specific purpose. God had a specific message for Abraham, for Moses, and for the others to whom He appeared. Each had no doubt about what God was trying to communicate.

God Communicates to Us in Many Ways

When God wanted to communicate specific messages, it was not necessary for Him to appear in person. He also spoke through the mouth of a prophet. The man of God would open his mouth and say, "Thus says the Lord." God would take control of his mind and mouth. In fact, sometimes in studying the Prophets it is impossible to isolate God from the prophet who spoke.

Take Deuteronomy 18:18, for example: "I will raise up for them a Prophet like you from among their brethren, and will put My words in His mouth, and He shall speak to them all that I command Him." Here is a prophecy concerning Christ, but it also pictures a human prophet.

The commission of Jeremiah as a prophet is another example: "Then the LORD put forth His hand and touched my mouth, and the LORD said to me: 'Behold, I have put My words in your mouth.' " (Jer. 1:9). When Jeremiah opened his mouth, God's Word came out.

It is also amazing to notice other ways God put His messages across. Sometimes He communicated by the casting of lots. God wanted Jonah to take a short ride in a long fish, and God wanted to make sure it would happen that way. So the pagan sailors on board the sinking ship cast lots, and the lot fell on Jonah. God made sure Jonah got the short stick.

Another fascinating way God communicated to His people was through use of the Urim and the Thummim, though no one today quite knows what these objects were. All we know is that they fit into the breastplate of the high priest—perhaps they were beautiful stones or jewelry (Lev. 8:8). Somehow they were used to tell the will of God (Ezra 2:63; 1 Sam. 28:6).

God also communicated through dreams, as in the case of Jacob (Gen. 28:12–15), Joseph (37:5–10), the butler and baker (40:5–23), and Pharaoh (41:1–44).

Another very common way for God to communicate was through visions. Daniel had both dreams and visions to learn the will and purposes of God.

At times God communicated by speaking audibly. For example, God said to Abraham, "Get out of your country; From your family; And from your father's house; To a land that I will show you" (Gen. 12:1).

Think of the apostle Paul on his way to Damascus. All of a sudden the Lord talked to him from out of heaven. What a fantastic concept. God could send His voice across the sky, from heaven, to communicate with spoken words.

The Means of a Miracle

In addition to communicating through nature and prophecy, God spoke through miracles. Simply defined, a miracle is an extraordinary event manifesting God's intervention so that God may reveal Himself in a special way.

Jesus verified His teaching with miracles so people could know He was God. The entire Gospel of John supports this. Jesus healed the lame man as easily as He forgave the man's sins (Mark 2:1–12). Only God could do that. This miracle demonstrated and authenticated that Jesus is God.

God used miracles to attest the truth of what He had said through His prophets. Elijah, for example, could announce what God had said, but it didn't mean anyone would listen. Some might ask, "How do we know you're telling the truth?" But when God empowered Elijah to raise somebody from the dead, it would inspire confidence that God was truly at work through his prophets (see 1 Kings 17:17–24).

Peter preached the gospel. Then he demonstrated divine power by healing the sick. That made people say, "This man must really be from God."

We see, in the New Testament accounts especially, that God accompanied His Word with signs in order that people might know it was His Word. In 2 Corinthians 12:12 we read about signs and wonders and the mighty deeds of the apostles that were used to certify the Word of God.

Any miracle testifies that God exists. It is one way God lets us know, "I am here, and I have something to say."

We should note that it isn't a problem for God to perform a miracle. He made the world, didn't He? For God, a miracle is like sticking His finger into a pond and making waves. And when God does a miracle, it doesn't create havoc in nature until the end of time, until Jesus comes back. It is self-contained. For example, Jesus stood at the tomb and said, "Lazarus, come forth," and Lazarus came out and took off his grave clothes. But later he would die again (John 11:43).

In his book *The Life of Jesus*, Ernest Renan says that he regards Bible miracles as legends. To him, the raising of Lazarus is a hypothesis: Lazarus was never dead; the people of Bethany only spoke of Lazarus as if he had been raised from the dead. Renan further calls the story of Lazarus a tradition. He is convinced that if we know the inaccuracies and the incoherent fables, which were part of the gossip of an ancient Middle Eastern city, then we must admit that a rumor of this kind was possible. At times he even infers that the family at Bethany was guilty of some type of indiscretion. Apparently Renan is implying that the family wanted people to believe in Jesus so much that they had Lazarus pretend he was dead in order to set up a phony resurrection. He even suggests that Lazarus may have had someone place him in the tomb, while Mary and Martha acted as if he was dead to go along with the ruse.

For All to See

Miracles do stand—and so do all the other means through which God has chosen to reveal Himself. They are recorded for us in the Bible, the embodiment of God's self-disclosure.

Jesus never healed anyone, Renan says. According to Renan, Jesus only aided sick people by His gentleness so that they felt better. Yet His followers considered these actions as miracles. At the Sea of Galilee, according to Renan, Jesus was not walking on water but was stepping on a very heavy growth of lily pads.

How did the feeding of the five thousand occur? Renan declares that a large quantity of food was stored in a nearby cave. Jesus knew about it and ordered His disciples to sneak it out.

It takes more faith to believe Renan's explanations than it does to accept the Bible record as it stands.

Isaiah, in his day, even with all that God had said to the prophets in those days, wanted more: "Truly You are God, who hide Yourself . . . Oh, that You would rend the heavens! That You would come down" (Is. 45:15; 64:1). And God did what Isaiah asked:

> God, who at various times and in various ways spoke in time past to the fathers by the prophets, has in these last days spoken to us by His Son, whom He has appointed heir of all things, through whom also He made the worlds; who being the brightness of His glory and the express image of His person, and upholding all things by the word of His power, when He had by Himself purged our sins, sat down at the right hand of the Majesty on high. (Heb. 1:1–3)

This becomes clear in the next aspect of our study. (Consult a Bible reference tool, such as the *MacArthur Study Bible,* for more on how God inspires the Scripture.)

Chapter Three
How Did God Inspire the Bible?

Revelation and inspiration are not the same. Revelation is the message, and inspiration was the primary method of delivering that message to mankind. Inspiration is the act of the Holy Spirit in revealing to human writers the message that God intended to comprise the Old and New Testaments.

In order to make this definition clear, let us look at what inspiration is *not*. First, *inspiration is not a high level of human achievement*. Think of Homer's *Odyssey*, Mohammed's *Koran*, Dante's *Divine Comedy*, or Shakespeare's tragedies. Some people say that the Bible is inspired in the same way that those great works of literature were inspired. In other words, the Bible is just the product of genius. The Bible is the result of natural inspiration; therefore, it has errors in it. It has fallible material which we can't believe. These people acknowledge that the Bible has high ethics and morals and great insights into humanity; but it is, after all, only a human achievement on the same level as other great writings.

The problem with that view is it is saying that God didn't write the Bible—smart men did. Would smart men write a book that condemns men to hell? Would smart men write a book that provides no human means of salvation apart from the perfect sacrifice of Jesus Christ? No! Man writes books that exalt himself. He doesn't write books to damn himself. The Bible cannot be understood as simply a product of human achievement.

Second, *inspiration is not only in the thoughts of the writers*. Some say that instead of giving the writers specific words, God supplied the writers only general ideas, while the choice of vocabulary was theirs. This view pictures God zapping Paul with a thought about how nice love is; and then in response, the apostle sat down and wrote

1 Corinthians 13. According to this view, the writers of Scripture were free to say what they wanted. That is why, though the overall truths of Scripture are divinely inspired, mistakes do appear in the Bible.

That view doesn't square with what the Bible teaches. Paul wrote, "We also speak, not in words which man's wisdom teaches but which the Holy Spirit teaches" (1 Cor. 2:13). The "words" are the words of the Spirit, Paul declared. Inspiration was not only in concepts and in thoughts, but in words as well.

Jesus said, "I have given to them the words which You have given Me" (John 17:8). Some 3,808 times in the Old Testament, expressions such as "Thus says the Lord," "The Word of the Lord," and "The Word of God" appear. These hardly express wordless concepts. God does communicate in words.

Take the case of Moses. When Moses tried to excuse himself from God's call on the basis of a speech problem, God didn't say, "I will inspire your thoughts." Rather, He promised, "I will be with your mouth and with his mouth, and I will teach you what you shall do" (Ex. 4:15). God didn't inspire thoughts; He inspired words.

That is why forty years later Moses was so insistent on giving verbatim instructions to the people of Israel: "You shall not add to the word which I command you, nor take from it, that you may keep the commandments of the LORD your God which I command you" (Deut. 4:2). "Don't add to the word and don't take away from the word," Moses was saying. Why? "Because God gave me these specific words for you," Moses would answer.

From the Holy Spirit

One of the greatest arguments against "thought inspiration" is found in 1 Peter where we read this about the work of the Old Testament prophets:

> Of this salvation the prophets have inquired and searched carefully, who prophesied of the grace that would come to you, searching

> what, or what manner of time, the Spirit of Christ who was in them was indicating when He testified beforehand the sufferings of Christ and the glories that would follow. (1 Pet. 1:10, 11)

The Spirit gave prophecies to the writers who wrote them down, read them, and tried to figure out what they meant. You might ask what is so amazing about that.

The amazing part about it is the prophets received words without understanding them. They recorded what they were told, but they didn't fully understand what they were writing. God didn't give them thoughts that they then expressed in their own words. God gave them the words. This is why pronouns, prepositions, and conjunctions, those parts of speech that seem insignificant, are important in the Bible. Jesus said, "Heaven and earth will pass away, but My words will by no means pass away" (Matt. 24:35).

The exchange between Peter and Christ supports the word-inspiration idea. When Peter said, "You are the Christ, the Son of the living God," Jesus answered, "Flesh and blood has not revealed this to you, but My Father who is in heaven" (Matt. 16:16, 17). Peter was speaking right off the top of his head what God was revealing in his mind. God gave him specific words, not just thoughts.

One writer has said, "Thoughts are wedded to words as soul to body." As far as thoughts being inspired apart from the words which give them expression, we might as well talk about a tune without notes or a sum without figures. We cannot have geology without rocks or anthropology without men. We cannot have a melody without music or a divine record of God without words. Thoughts are carried by words, and God revealed His thoughts in words. We call that verbal inspiration.

Goose-bump Theology

There is a third thing that inspiration is *not. Inspiration is not the act of God on the reader.* There are some who teach what we could call existential inspiration, which means that the only part of the Bible that is inspired is the part that zaps you. You read along and you get "goose bumps," meaning that a particular word or passage is inspired for *you*. It becomes God's Word when it hits you. If you get ecstatic and emotional, convicted or confronted, then it is God's Word to you. But if you sit there unresponsive, it is not the Word of God. It is not authoritative.

There are those who say there are myths in Scripture and try to "demythologize" the Bible. They want to eliminate what they think is untrue. With this reasoning or approach, they may edit out Christ's preexistence, virgin birth, deity, miracles, substitutionary death, resurrection, and ascension. They may maintain that all of that is historically false. To reject the historical character of Scripture and maintain that it can still say something spiritually meaningful and can come from God doesn't make sense. If the Bible lies from beginning to end about history, why should we believe its spiritual message? If the Bible is lying when its recorded events are verifiable in history, why should we believe it in its spiritual content when we can't easily verify it? It seems to me that if God wants us to trust the spiritual character of the Bible, He would make sure that the historical character of the Bible is trustworthy.

Jesus said, "Your word is truth" (John 17:17). Inspiration is not the inspiration of the reader.

To conclude what inspiration is not: *Inspiration is not mechanical dictation.* The Bible writers were not robots, writing in a semicomatose state, cranking it out without using their minds.

It is true that God could have used dictation to give us the truth—He didn't have to use men. God could have spoken His Word into existence and dropped it on us like revelatory rain. But we know that He didn't do it that way because when we open the Bible, we find personality. Every book has a different character. Each author has a unique style. There are variations in language and vocabulary. And when we read the various books of the Bible, we can feel the emotions the writers were experiencing at the time.

At Work in the Writer

But how can the Bible be the Word of God and at the same time, for example, the words of Paul? God formed the personality of the writer. God made Paul into the man He wanted him to be. God controlled his heredity and his environment. When the writer reached the point that God intended, God directed and controlled the free choice of the man so that he wrote down the very words of God. God literally selected the words out of each author's own life, out of his personality, his vocabulary, and his emotions. The words were man's words, but that man's life had been so framed by God that they were God's words as well. So we can say that Paul wrote Romans, and we can say God wrote it. Both statements are correct.

David testified, "The Spirit of the LORD spoke by me, and His word was on my tongue" (2 Sam. 23:2). It came out as God's Word. Thrilling! Holy men of God were moved along by the Holy Spirit (2 Pet. 1:21). They were authors, not secretaries. They wrote out of their personalities. We read Jeremiah, the weeping prophet, and we can feel his emotion. We read about the fires of judgment expressed by Amos, and we can almost experience it. Personality comes through every part of Scripture.

To sum up, inspiration is not a high level of human achievement; it is not confined to thoughts alone; it is not the act of God on the reader; and it is not mechanical dictation.

To understand the real meaning of inspiration, we need to look at a key passage on the subject. "All Scripture is given by inspiration of God" (2 Tim. 3:16). That could be translated, "All Scripture is God-breathed" because the Greek word *theopneustos* comes from the words God and *breath.* The expression means that which comes out of God's mouth—His Word.

As we study the doctrine of inspiration, we discover that this is the method by which God has spoken. Earlier we saw that natural revelation came about by the breath of God: "By the word of the LORD the heavens were made; and all the host of them by the breath of His mouth" (Ps. 33:6). God breathed the universe into existence. Then God breathed the Bible into existence. Special revelation comes about in the same way natural revelation did—by the breath of God. Whatever the Scriptures say, God said. Sometimes the word "Scripture" is used in place of the word "God." "And the Scripture . . . preached the gospel to Abraham beforehand, saying, 'In you all the nations shall be blessed.'" (Gal. 3:8). And, "the *Scripture has confined* all under sin, that the promise by faith in Jesus Christ might be given to those who believe" (Gal. 3:22, author's italics). Here the Bible speaks and acts as the voice of God.

We find the same in the Old Testament. In Exodus we read that God said to Pharaoh, "But indeed for this purpose I have raised you up, that I may show My power in you, and that My name may be declared in all the earth" (9:16). That is God speaking. Paul referred to this conversation in Romans 9:17, but he wrote, "For the *Scripture says* to Pharaoh, "For this very purpose I have raised you up" (author's italics). When the Scripture speaks, God speaks. When God speaks, the Scripture speaks. In every sense, when you pick up the Bible and read it, you are hearing God's voice. This is exciting. God is the author of what Scripture records. The Bible is the very Word of God.

From Him through Them to Us

The Bible writers in both the Old and New Testaments were commissioned to write the revelation of God in God's own words. Isaiah had a vision of the Lord sitting on His throne. He wrote, "I heard the voice of the Lord, saying, 'Whom shall I send, And who will go for us?'" (Is. 6:8). Isaiah recorded the words of God.

The prophet Jeremiah wrote, "Then the word of the LORD came to me, saying: 'Before I formed you in the womb I knew you; Before you were born I sanctified you; I ordained you a prophet to the nations'" (Jer. 1:4, 5). "Then the LORD put forth His hand and touched my mouth, and the LORD said to me: 'Behold, I have put My words in your mouth.' " (v. 9). What would be the result? "Because you speak this word, Behold, I will make My words in your mouth fire, And this people wood, And it shall devour them" (5:14). That is vivid!

Ezekiel testified time after time that he spoke the words God had given him. God said to His prophet, "Son of man, receive into your heart all My words that I speak to you, and hear with your ears. And go, get to the captives, to the children of your people, and speak to them and tell them, 'Thus says the Lord GOD' " (Ezek. 3:10, 11). And he did.

Paul wrote to the Galatians that it was God who gave him his message: "But when it pleased God, who separated me from my mother's womb and called me through His grace, to reveal His Son in me, that I might preach Him among the Gentiles, I did not immediately confer with flesh and blood" (Gal. 1:15, 16). Paul did not get his message from his fellow apostles—it came directly from God.

Think of the disciple John. Is the Book of Revelation something he conceived? Never. "I was in the Spirit on the Lord's Day, and I heard behind me a loud voice, as of a trumpet, saying, . . . 'What you see, write in a book and send it to the seven churches' " (Rev. 1:10, 11).

All these Bible writers—and the others as well—gave clear-cut evidence that what they wrote was from God; it was the breath of God. This is one essential factor of inspiration.

Some, Most, or All?

But now the question arises, "How much of Scripture is God-breathed?" Let's return to 2 Timothy 3:16 and check out another Greek word: "*All* Scripture is given by inspiration of God." The word "all"—*pasa* in the Greek—can be translated "every." So we see that *all* Scripture and every Scripture is inspired.

Consider this analogy: All ducks waddle. Does that mean that only ducks of the past waddle? No. Ducks still waddle today. What about future ducks? Future ducks will also waddle. In other words, in whatever period of history ducks live, ducks waddle.

Here is the point: To say Scripture is God-breathed means *all* Scripture, regardless of when it was written, is God-breathed.

This unity of the Scripture as a body of truth was taught by the Lord Jesus when He said, "Scripture cannot be broken" (John 10:35). All Scripture is pure and authentic. None can be violated. The Lord meant *all* that had been written, *all* that was being written, and *all* that would be written. All of Scripture is the holy writings of God.

There is a third Greek word we need to examine. It is *graphe* from which we get the term graphite—the lead in a pencil. *Graphe*, then, means "writing"—all *writing,* all Scripture is inspired. Paul wrote to Timothy, "And how from childhood you have known the sacred writings that are able to instruct you for salvation through faith in Christ Jesus" (2 Tim. 3:15, NRSV). When we talk about "writing" being inspired, we are talking about the Scriptures only—the "sacred writings."

There is a point here that we might miss. What is it that is inspired? The writers? No, the writings. Paul was not inspired, but that which he wrote, the Book of Romans, was inspired. And that is true of the other letters that he wrote as well. They were inspired, but not the author. "All *Scripture*," said Paul.

The Bible never says that Moses was inspired, or David, or Paul—not the men, but the message was inspired. That is why a man could write an inspired message at one period in his life and perhaps no other message during the remainder of his life.

Despite that teaching, however, we have people today who want to remove this verse or some other verse from Scripture. They want to decide what stays and what goes. The principle they follow is something they call the "spirit of Jesus." Whatever in the Bible fits the spirit of Jesus, they accept. Whatever doesn't fit the spirit of Jesus, they reject.

Perhaps these people are reading in the New Testament and come across the account of our Lord's cleansing of the temple. They want to deny that this incident took place, rationalizing that it is not really a part of Scripture because it isn't from the meek and loving spirit of

Jesus. Their concept of Jesus is a wimpish character who is so meek and gentle that He has no sense of judgment or justice. They make Jesus what they wish, and they throw out of Scripture anything that doesn't conform to their "fantasy Jesus."

But Jesus said, "For assuredly, I say to you, till heaven and earth pass away, one jot or one tittle will by no means pass from the law till all is fulfilled" (Matt. 5:18). The Greek words refer to a very small mark, similar in size to our punctuation marks, placed under a word like a dot or a comma. Not one mark will be removed. It is not to be touched—it is that serious. Yet there are people going through the Bible cutting out whole passages.

Warnings in the Word

Jesus warns, "Whoever therefore breaks one of the least of these commandments, and teaches men so, shall be called least in the kingdom of heaven" (Matt. 5:19). God doesn't want anyone tampering with His words.

What would it take to change the Word of God? "It is easier for heaven and earth to pass away than for one tittle of the law to fail" (Luke 16:17). It is easier for the entire universe to fold up than for the smallest mark in the Bible to be altered. God's Word is eternal!

This doesn't mean that men won't tamper with it. Jesus told the Pharisees that they had "invalidated" the Word of God by their tradition which they had handed down (Mark 7:13, NASB). They had destroyed the effectiveness of Scripture by their additions and misinterpretations. In setting aside a part, they were in effect, casting aside the whole, for the Bible is a unit that is not meant to be broken.

"The entirety of Your word is truth; and every one of Your righteous judgments endures forever" (Ps. 119:160). Another important passage bears on this matter: "No prophecy of Scripture is of any private interpretation, for prophecy never came by the will of man, but holy men of God spoke as they were moved by the Holy Spirit" (2 Pet. 1:20, 21). This refers to origin. Scripture did not originate privately. It didn't come out of a man's mind, but by men carried along by the Holy Spirit.

"But this verse is talking only about prophecy," someone may point out.

Yes, but prophecy isn't only prediction. Genesis, Exodus, Leviticus, Numbers, and Deuteronomy are prophecies. These books, called the Pentateuch, were written by Moses, and Moses was a prophet.

There are predictions to the coming Messiah in them, but basically those books are history. Prophecy doesn't have to be predictive. Prophecy means "speaking" or "telling forth." It is a communication from God; and all communication from God came, not by the will of man, but by men used by God as they were borne along by the Holy Spirit.

Inspiration is God's revelation communicated to us through writers who used their own minds and their own words. God had so arranged their lives, their thoughts, and their vocabularies that the words they chose were the words that God determined from eternity past that they would use to write His truth.

That's a miracle! Theologians call it the plenary verbal inspiration of Scripture. Plenary means all. Nothing is missing. Verbal means word. So every word in the Bible is God-breathed.

What logically follows from this definition? First, the Bible is *infallible.* It speaks only the truth. If God wrote it, it has to be true. "The Law of the LORD is perfect" (Ps. 19:7).

No Mistakes

In addition to being perfect, the Bible is also *inerrant* in the original manuscripts—the Bible has no mistakes. It is true that as the Bible has come down to us through the generations, there may be slight variations in the manuscripts. These are apparent and generally known to us. But basically, we can look at the totality of the Word of God and say, "This is, as it was in the original language, the Word of God." Even as He upholds the world by His power, so He upholds the Bible in an infallible state.

That should caution us again about tampering with the Word of God. We read, "Do not add to His words; lest He rebuke you, and you be found a liar" (Prov. 30:6). When anyone wants to add a new revelation or claim new inspiration, that person falls into the category of those described in Revelation 22:

> For I testify to everyone who hears the words of the prophecy of this book: If anyone adds to these things, God will add to him the plagues that are written in this book; and if anyone takes away from the words of the book of this prophecy, God shall take away his part from the Book of Life, from the holy city, and from the things which are written in this book. (Rev. 22:18, 19)

No More Needed

In addition to being infallible and inerrant, Scripture is also *complete*. The Bible is all that we need to have a right relationship with God. We don't need a vision. We don't need a new revelation or a voice from heaven. The Scriptures are "the faith which was once for all delivered to the saints" (Jude 3).

The New Testament books demanded (for their authentication) authorship by an apostle or someone close to an apostle. The apostles were the foundation of the church (Eph. 2:20). In the twentieth century, the foundation is not being relaid. There are no more apostles; therefore, there are no more revelations. Today we enjoy the illumination of Scripture by the Holy Spirit, not by contemporary inspiration.

The Word of God is also *authoritative*. When it speaks, we had better respond. "Hear, O heavens, and give ear, O earth; for the LORD has spoken" (Is. 1:2). That says it all. This is God's voice recorded in Scripture, and we'd better listen to it.

The Bible is *sufficient*. Because the Word of God is the breath of God, we don't need anything more. Go back again to that basic text,

"All Scripture is given by inspiration of God, and is profitable for doctrine, for reproof, for correction, for instruction in righteousness, that the man of God may be complete, thoroughly equipped for every good work" (2 Tim. 3:16, 17). The King James Version says, "That the man of God may be perfect." Is there anything needed beyond perfection? Is anything missing? When we say the Bible is sufficient, we mean nothing is missing. Paul wrote that Timothy from childhood had known the sacred writings which were able to give him the wisdom that leads to salvation through faith which is in Christ Jesus (2 Tim. 3:15). The Bible is all anyone needs to find salvation and to become mature in Christ.

If a person ever troubles you by saying you need this spiritual or mystical experience or that one, don't believe it. The Spirit of God acting through the Word of God is sufficient to make you fully mature in Christ.

We have said that the Bible is infallible, inerrant, complete, authoritative, and sufficient. The Bible is also *effective*. "For the word of God is living and powerful, and sharper than any two-edged sword, piercing even to the division of soul and spirit, and of joints and marrow, and is a discerner of the thoughts and intents of the heart" (Heb. 4:12). God said, "So shall My word be that goes forth from My mouth; It shall not return to Me void; but it shall accomplish what I please, and it shall prosper in the thing for which I sent it" (Is. 55:11). And Paul said to the Thessalonians, "For our gospel did not come to you in word only, but also in power, and in the Holy Spirit and in much assurance" (1 Thess. 1:5).

The Word of God is effective—all believers have experienced this in their lives. The Bible is a powerful book. It tears me up, and it puts me back together again. Take the Word of God and the Spirit of God together; and you have dynamite.

One of the reasons I know God wrote the Bible is that it tells me things about myself that only He and I know, and usually at a depth I didn't understand before. And then through the Word He rearranges me to be what He wants me to be.

Beloved, we are to stand faithfully and carefully on this inspired Word of God, which is infallible, inerrant, complete, authoritative, sufficient, and effective. But there are many people who don't. Our Lord tells us why: "He who is of God hears God's words; therefore you do not hear, because you are not of God" (John 8:47).

One way to tell a saved person from an unsaved one is that one listens to the Word of God and the other doesn't. Are you listening? Are you studying the Bible with resources like the *MacArthur Study Bible*? The effort is well worth it, for the Bible is God's Word to you.

Chapter Four

What Does the Bible Say about Itself?

Imagine you are in a court of law and the Bible is on trial. You are counsel for the defense. What witnesses can you call to give testimony to the truthfulness and the authoritative infallibility of the Bible?

I think I would appeal to at least three different sources. The first would be the Bible writers themselves, the human instruments through which the revelation was given. Two Bible writers were kings. Two were priests. One was a physician. Two were fishermen. Two were shepherds. Paul was a Pharisee and a theologian. Daniel was a statesman. Matthew was a tax collector. Joshua was a soldier. Ezra was a scribe. Nehemiah was a butler. The list goes on.

As we begin to take the testimony of the 40 or more writers who wrote over a period of 1,600 years, we discern a common air of infallibility, beginning with Moses who wrote the Pentateuch and ending with the apostle John who wrote Revelation. With a few exceptions they were the simplest kind of men, without formal education, yet these fishermen, farmers, shepherds, and a tax collector were confident that they were setting down the Word of God.

That is astounding. Several thousand times in the Bible, in one way or another, these men who wrote the Bible claimed to be writing the Word of God.

If I were to sit down and write something and announce, "This is the revelation of God," people would say, "Who do you think you are?" I would be very self-conscious about making any declaration that what I had written was God's Word—but not the Bible writers. There is no self-consciousness, no effort to convince us that they were really relating the Word of God. They made the claim, and that settled it.

No Apologies

You will not find in the Bible any statement such as these: "Friends, this may sound ridiculous, but this is the Word of God." "You may find this very hard to believe, but God actually gave me these words."

Recall how Peter was in Jerusalem preaching and firing off all kinds of wonderful messages when He was hauled before the Sanhedrin for trial. Did he say, "Now I realize that we are ignorant and unlearned Galileans. I know you're not going to believe us. But what do you think? Can we speak God's Word to you?"

Of course not. There was an air of authority about Peter's preaching, an infallibility to his witness. He could boldly declare, "Nor is there salvation in any other, for there is no other name under heaven given among men by which we must be saved" (Acts 4:12).

All the Bible writers wrote with the same authority. Though they lived in different times and circumstances, they wove a perfect theme that never contradicts itself, that is, in fact, the Word of God.

These writers touched on many areas. The Bible contains history that can be verified. The Bible contains science, which is factually correct, "He hangs the earth on nothing" (Job 26:7). The Bible talks about medicine and gives laws of health. Doctors today can verify that the Bible has information that can contribute to a healthy life. There is also commentary on ethics in the Bible; and there is practical wisdom essential to leading a happy life.

Sometimes it takes scientists a long time to catch up with what the Bible has been saying all along. It wasn't until the sixteenth century that William Harvey discovered the workings of the circulatory system in the human body. Yet the first book in the Bible declares that the life of the flesh is in the blood (Gen. 9:4).

Herbert Spencer, who died in 1903, announced that everything in the universe fits into five categories—time, force, action, space, and matter. Everybody said, "Wonderful." But Moses wrote in the first verse of the Bible, "In the beginning [time] God [force] created [action] the heaven [space] and the earth [matter]" (Gen. 1:1).

Then there is prophecy. For example, the Bible predicted that Babylon, the greatest city of the ancient world, would be destroyed. At the time, that statement was scorned as irresponsible—it was comparable to saying that the Boy Scouts would demolish New York. It couldn't happen. Yet Babylon was destroyed just as the Bible said. Such examples are numerous.

The only reasonable source for such vast amounts of information was certainly outside the writers. If God didn't write the Bible, then who did? Mere men acting on their own could never have done it.

His Word

What are the claims of Bible writers? Let's call the Old Testament authors into our courtroom and ask them. They refer to their writings as the words of God 3,808 times. Once would be enough, but 3,808 times is more than sufficient. This amount of testimony builds a substantial case.

From Psalms 19 and 119, for example, come such statements as "The Law of the LORD is perfect" (Ps. 19:17). "I hope in Your Word" (Ps. 119:81). "Your Word is very pure" (Ps. 119:140). "Your Law is truth" (Ps. 119:142). "All Your commandments are truth" (Ps. 119:151). "Every one of Your righteous judgments endures forever" (Ps. 119:162). "My tongue shall speak of Your Word; for all Your commandments are righteousness" (Ps. 119:172).

The prophet Amos testified, "Surely the Lord GOD does nothing; unless He reveals His secret to His servants the prophets" (3:7). God told His prophets what He was going to do, and the testimony of these Old Testament writers is that God breathed the very words of the Bible.

What about the New Testament writers? Did they believe what the Old Testament writers believed? At least 320 quotations in the New

Testament come directly out of the Old Testament. Check, for example, the words of Paul: "For whatever things were written before [the Old Testament] were written for our learning, that we through the patience and comfort of the Scriptures might have hope" (Rom. 15:4). Paul considered the Old Testament writings Scripture.

Peter said that holy men of God wrote as they were borne along by the Holy Spirit (2 Pet. 1:21). Peter believed that the Old Testament was inspired. The writer of Hebrews said that "God, who at various times and in various ways spoke in time past to the fathers by the prophets" (Heb. 1:1). That writer believed the Old Testament was the Word of God. James, in a passage describing the authority of the Old Testament writings, called them "Scripture" (James 4:5).

The Witness of Acts

There are many illustrations of how New Testament writers referred to the Old Testament, and indicated their belief that God wrote it. Consider these in the Book of Acts.

In his sermon Peter said, "Men and brethren, this Scripture had to be fulfilled, which the Holy Spirit spoke before by the mouth of David concerning Judas, who became a guide to those who arrested Jesus" (Acts 1:16). This is a conclusive statement that the Old Testament was equally inspired by the Holy Spirit. In fact, Peter was saying that the Holy Spirit used David's mouth to speak. This is a New Testament writer's view of the Old Testament inspiration.

In Acts 4:25 is another example: "Who by the mouth of Your servant David have said." A better translation would be, "Who, by the Holy Spirit through the mouth of Your servant David, have said." Here is a quotation from the Old Testament that is not only assigned to David but also to the Holy Spirit. So again we find that the Christians in the early church believed that what came through David's mouth was equally the Word of God.

These are only two illustrations from Acts underscoring the fact that the New Testament writers believed that the words of the prophets in the Old Testament Scriptures were in fact the words of the Holy Spirit. There are many other examples that we could cite.

The Witness of the New Testament

A further element concerns us. Do New Testament writers ever say that other New Testament writers are inspired? Is there any testimony from New Testament writers about other New Testament writers? A verse from 1 Timothy sets us off on an exciting investigation: "For the Scripture says, 'You shall not muzzle an ox while it treads out the grain,' and, 'The laborer is worthy of his wages'" (5:18). We read that first principle in Deuteronomy 25:4. Paul quotes that verse and calls it "Scripture," and then goes on to say, "The laborer is worthy of his wages," which are the words of the Lord Jesus recorded in Luke 10:7. In one verse, Paul is saying that both the Old Testament and the New Testament are Scripture. So here is a New Testament writer corroborating the New Testament as Scripture.

The Book of 1 Peter provides further support:

> And consider that the longsuffering of our Lord is salvation—as also our beloved brother Paul, according to the wisdom given to him, has written to you, as also in all his epistles, speaking in them of these things, in which are some things hard to understand, which untaught and unstable people twist to their own destruction, as they do also the rest of the Scriptures. (1 Pet. 3:15, 16)

Peter was saying, "I'm telling you what our beloved Paul said." In doing that, Peter declared that all of Paul's letters are Scripture and do what the other Scriptures do—instruct us in the ways of God. What Paul wrote was as much the Word of God as the Old Testament. This is one of the great statements on New Testament inspiration. It covers Romans, 1 and 2 Corinthians, Galatians, Ephesians, Philippians, Colossians, 1 and 2 Thessalonians, 1 and 2 Timothy, Titus, and Philemon.

What about John and the Book of Revelation? At the beginning of each message to the seven churches John testified, "These things says He," referring to the Lord Jesus (Rev. 2:1). He also wrote, "Let him hear what the Spirit says" (Rev. 2:7). John was saying that all of Revelation was coming from Jesus Christ through him and that the whole is the message of the Holy Spirit. Throughout Revelation John included such expressions as "These are the true sayings of God" (Rev. 19:9), and "These words are true and faithful" (Rev. 21:5).

Taken together, we have established the fact that the Gospels, the Epistles, and the Book of Revelation were inspired by God. The testimony of the New Testament writers was that they were writing the Word of God.

Jesus and the Record

In addition to the testimony of the writers themselves, we have a second witness—the Lord Jesus Christ. He had a number of vital things to say about Scripture. He declared that He was the theme of all Scripture. Jesus said to the Jewish leaders, "You search the Scriptures, for in them you think you have eternal life; and these are they which testify of Me" (John 5:39).

Not only did Christ teach that He was the theme of all Scripture, but He also said that He came to fulfill all Scripture. He said, "Do not think that I came to destroy the Law or the Prophets. I did not come to destroy but to fulfill" (Matt. 5:17). He looked at His cross and said, "The Son of Man indeed goes just as it is written of Him" (Matt. 26:24). He told Peter that He didn't need the protection of his sword, for if He wished He could call down thousands of angels for assistance. "But how then could the Scriptures be fulfilled, that it must happen thus?" (Matt. 26:54). Jesus came to fulfill Scripture. He saw Scripture as pointing to His own life and death; every detail of it had to be fulfilled.

In a strong statement concerning Scripture, Jesus said, "Scripture cannot be broken" (John 10:35). He meant that what God said was true and what was prophesied in Scripture would take place. He even compared the duration of Scripture to the duration of the universe. He said, "It is easier for heaven and earth to pass away than for one tittle of the law to fail" (Luke 16:17). "All things that are written by the prophets . . . will be accomplished" (Luke 18:31).

Jesus' view of Scripture then was that it was the Word of God and that what was written was certain to come to pass. He even called attention to individual words.

David predicted that when the Messiah died on the cross, He would cry out, "My God, My God, why have You forsaken Me? (Ps. 22:1). While dying on the cross, Jesus cried out, "My God, My God, why have You forsaken Me?" (Matt. 27:46). Psalm 22 also foretold that the suffering Savior would feel thirsty. On the cross Jesus cried out, "I thirst" (John 19:28).

Jesus believed in every word of the Old Testament. He corroborated the great truths of the Old Testament. For example, He confirmed the creation of Adam and Eve, in effect stating that what the Old Testament says about them is true. He said, "Have you not read that He who made them at the beginning 'made them male and female,' and said, 'For this reason a man shall leave his father and mother and be joined to his wife, and the two shall become one flesh'?" (Matt. 19:4, 5). Jesus believed that God created the universe as recorded in Genesis.

Jesus substantiated many other facts in the Book of Genesis—such as the destruction of Sodom and Gomorrah and the turning of Lot's wife into a pillar of salt. In Mark 12 we read that He affirmed the call of Moses; and in John 6 He talked about the manna from heaven. He referred to the brazen serpent lifted up in the wilderness by which Israel was healed (John 3). Over and over again, Jesus confirmed the authority of the Old Testament record.

Jesus also established the sufficiency of the Scripture to save men. In the account of the rich man and Lazarus, the Lord quoted Abraham from the perspective of Paradise, saying, "They have Moses and the prophets; let them hear them" (Luke 16:29). He was saying that the brothers of Lazarus didn't need one to rise from the dead in order for them to be saved. The testimony of the prophets was sufficient to bring them to the knowledge of the truth.

Jesus also spoke of the ability of Scriptures to keep one from error, referring to those who had erred as doing so because they didn't know the Scriptures (Mark 12:24, 27).

There is an interesting statistic about the Lord's use of Old Testament Scriptures. Of the 1,800 verses in the New Testament which include quotations of Jesus, 180 of them, or one-tenth, come from the Old Testament. He who is the Truth, who is the Word, believed and submitted to the inspired writings of the Old Testament without reservation. If Jesus was committed to that, I'm certainly willing to be. If Jesus believed in the Old Testament Scriptures, I believe them also.

The Final Witness

We have considered the witness of the Bible writers and the witness of Jesus. We must also call the Holy Spirit as a witness. The belief that the Bible is the inspired Word of God is not the result of an intellectual decision. Rather it is the result of the work of the Holy Spirit in a person's life. An individual won't believe the Bible until the Holy Spirit has done His work of convincing that person.

Let's sketch the argument. We believe the Bible is true because the Bible says it is true. "That's circular reasoning," someone objects. Good point. If a person doesn't believe the Bible, he is not going to believe the Bible when the Bible says that it is the Word of God. On the other hand, if a person accepts the Bible as the Word of God, it is because the work of the Holy Spirit caused that truth to dawn on him.

People are not so stupid that they can't understand the truth; they are hostile because they don't want to accept the truth. People do not want to include God in their knowledge, so when they hear the preaching of the Cross they consider it foolishness (1 Cor. 1:21). The natural (unregenerate) man doesn't receive the things of God (1 Cor. 2:14). In order for his abnormal and depraved mind to receive the truth of God, the Holy Spirit must work.

It is, therefore, impossible by argument, or by preaching alone, to cause someone to believe the Bible. Everyone is dependent on the internal work of the Spirit; but the Spirit cannot produce belief in the Word of God until a person has heard the Word of God. Paul asked, "How then shall they call on Him in whom they have not believed? And how shall they believe in Him of whom they have not heard? And how shall they hear without a preacher?" (Rom. 10:14).

Time for Decision

Our case is finished. We have looked at the testimonies of the Old Testament writers and of the New Testament writers, of the Lord Jesus Christ and of the Holy Spirit—all defending the inspiration of the Bible. It is a solid case. The only possible verdict is that the Scriptures are indeed God's inspired Word.

What should be our response to this fact? We must practice Colossians 3:16: "Let the Word of Christ dwell in you richly." Our minds should be a tablet where the Word of God is written. We are to read it and study it with the useful Bible resources available to us, such as the *MacArthur Study Bible* and other Bible commentaries. We are to obey it and apply all of its teachings to our lives. Then, we are to pass it on.

It has been estimated that in one lifetime the average citizen will consume 150 head of cattle, 2,400 chickens, 225 lambs, 26 sheep, 310 pigs, 26 acres of grain, and 50 acres of fruits and vegetables. That's a lot of food.

How much of the Word of God are you consuming? An outdoor bulletin board at a church in Quincy, Massachusetts carried this message: "A Bible that is falling apart usually belongs to someone who isn't."

You have in the Bible a genuine treasure.

Chapter Five
How Important Is the Bible?

How important is the Bible to me? There are several ways to answer that question. Some say, "The Bible? It's just another book. It has some wise sayings here and there, mixed with a lot of genealogies, myths, and crazy visions."

A second group says something like this: "Of course I know the Bible is important—at least my pastor thinks so. He's always quoting it and waving it in the air. But I don't read it too much. I can't understand it too well."

There is still a third group, however, who would align themselves with Sir Walter Scott, a famed British novelist and poet, who was also a committed Christian. On his deathbed Scott is reported to have said to his secretary, "Bring me the Book." His secretary thought of the thousands of books in Scott's library and inquired, "Dr. Scott, which book?" "The Book," replied Scott. "The Bible—the only book for a dying man!"

And the committed Christian would have to add that the Bible is not just the only book for a dying man, but it's the only book for a living man, because it is the Word of God.

In which of the three categories do you fall? Obviously Group 1 represents the typical response from the secular world. It doesn't know Christ; and it accepts only what seems to fit in with worldly wisdom. For them, the Bible has little importance and less authority.

Group 2 includes a lot of church members, and even some Christians. They know the Bible is important and that it should be a priority and an authority in their lives, but they don't make much personal use of it. They neglect its teachings altogether. Or they slip by, seldom opening the Bible for themselves, depending on pastors, teachers, or speakers to "explain it to them." They don't apply what the Scriptures teach. The Bible remains a mysterious, somewhat confusing rule book that they are supposed to swallow bravely, like castor oil, every morning before breakfast.

Group 3 sees the Bible much differently. For them the Scriptures are alive, literally popping with exciting truths. This group doesn't live by bread alone, "but by every word that proceeds from the mouth of God" (Matt. 4:4).

But perhaps you're thinking that you don't quite fit in any of these three categories. If you are like a lot of Christians, you land somewhere between Group 2 and Group 3. You want the Bible to become more important to you. You want to submit to its authority, but life crowds the Bible out. Everywhere you turn you are enticed, or intimidated, to forget the teachings of the Scripture.

For example, you turn on a television talk show and hear a big star making authoritative announcements, such as, "I think everyone should do his own thing, live his own life, and have his own faith." The studio audience bursts into applause; and you're left wondering if it's really very bright (or even American) to think that you, a born-again Christian and member of a church, have all the answers between the covers of such an old and seemingly "outdated" book.

But when we let the world's value system intimidate us, we forget a basic truth. In a world of relativistic thinking that has no absolutes, the Bible stands as the absolute authority for the Christian. The Scriptures are the Word of God, not someone's opinions, ideas, or philosophy. It isn't even a polling of the best thoughts from the best thinkers. Scripture is God's Word; and that means it has several characteristics and qualities that should make it extremely important in our lives.

God's Word Is Infallible

Some statements of faith published by churches or Christian organizations say, "The Bible is God's Word, the infallible rule of faith and practice." That is a good statement, but I prefer an even stronger one that says, "The Bible is God's *infallible* Word, the only rule of faith and practice." There is a real difference where you place the word *infallible* in those two statements. The second statement clearly says that *in its totality* the Bible makes no mistakes. The original autographs (the first copies) were without error. Copiers have made minor mistakes over the centuries, but none of these are serious enough to challenge the Bible's infallibility. The Bible says of itself, "The law of the LORD is perfect" (Ps. 19:7). The Bible is flawless because it was authored (or inspired) by a God who is flawless. I have already discussed inspiration of Scripture in detail, but the point to think about here is this: If God is our ultimate authority, and His character is flawless, and if He inspired the writers of Scripture to put down His thoughts while still allowing them freedom of personal expression, then the Bible is flawless and it becomes our ultimate authority—our only rule for faith and practice.

To put it another way, if we believe God is perfect it has to follow that the original copies of Scripture also had to be perfect. Is the Bible infallible? It has to be, because it is the only book that never makes a mistake.

God's Word Is Inerrant

The Bible is not only infallible in its totality but it is inerrant in all its parts. The writer of Proverbs says it well: "Every word of God is pure, He is a shield to those who put their trust in Him" (Prov. 30:5).

In regard to Scripture, inerrancy and infallibility go hand in hand. According to the writers of the Chicago Statement on Biblical Inerrancy, the negative terms infallible and inerrant "have special value, for they explicitly safeguard crucial positive truths." The Chicago Statement, drafted at a summit conference called in October 1978 by the International Council on Biblical Inerrancy to affirm the authority of Scripture, goes on to say:

> *Infallible* signifies the quality of neither misleading nor being misled and so safeguards in categorical terms the truth that Holy Scripture is a sure, safe, and reliable rule and guide in all matters.
>
> Similarly, *inerrant* signifies the quality of being free from all falsehood or mistake and so safeguards the truth that Holy Scripture is entirely true and trustworthy in all its assertions.[1]

As implied in both the above definitions, one convenient way to describe infallibility and inerrancy is in the word *truthfulness.* In Isaiah 65:16 the Lord calls Himself, "God of truth." In Jeremiah 10:10 the prophet writes, "The LORD is the true God." The New Testament agrees with the Old in calling God a God of truth. Examples of many such statements include: "God is true" (John 3:33); "the only true God" (John 17:3); "This is the true God" (1 John 5:20).

To make sure we don't overlook the importance of God' s truthfulness, three times the Scripture stresses that God cannot lie (see Num. 23:19; Titus 1:2; Heb. 6:18).

Some critics of Scripture, however, like to point out that biblical "truthfulness" is open to question because Scripture contains terms that are not scientifically precise or grammatically correct and passages that seem to contradict one another. The writers of the Chicago Statement face this criticism head on by saying:

> In determining what the God-taught writer is asserting in each passage, we must pay the most careful attention to its claims and character as a human production. In inspiration, God utilized the culture and conventions of his penman's milieu, a milieu that God controls in His sovereign providence; it is misinterpretation to imagine otherwise.
>
> So history must be treated as history, poetry as poetry, hyperbole and metaphor as hyperbole and metaphor, generalization and approximation as what they are, and so forth. Differences between literary conventions in Bible times and in ours must be observed . . . nonchronological narration and imprecise citation were conventional and acceptable and violated no expectations in those days . . . Scripture

is inerrant, not in the sense of being absolutely precise by modern standards, but in the sense of making good its claims and achieving that measure of focused truth at which its authors aimed.[2]

In a list of Twenty Articles of Affirmation and Denial, the Chicago Statement further confirms the need to understand how God inspired certain men to write Scripture at certain times, under certain circumstances. Article XIII reads: "We affirm the propriety of using inerrancy as a theological term with reference to the complete truthfulness of Scripture."[3]

Testimony for the truthfulness of God is found throughout His written Word, and if we don't accept and believe that testimony we will wind up somewhere in Group 2—those who know the Bible is supposed to be important, but who remain apathetic about what it says. In fact, such apathy can lead to real despair. A young man visited my office and said, "My whole Christian life is in a mess. Everything is falling apart. I can't study the Bible, I have these doubts."

I listened to him for about twenty minutes and then I said, "I can tell you right now what your problem is. It's obvious."

"What is it?" he wanted to know.

I replied, "You do not believe in the absolute inerrancy of Scripture. If you believe there are errors in the Word of God, then you become confused don't know what to believe. That's your problem."

"You know," he said, "you hit it right on the nose. I don't believe in the absolute inerrancy of Scripture."

"Then my friend," I answered, "how can you hope to be an effective student of the Word of God or to ever lead an effective Christian life?"

Is the Bible inerrant? It has to be, because the Bible is God' s Word and God is a God of truth.

God's Word Is Authoritative

If the Bible is infallible and inerrant, it must be the final word—the highest standard of authority. The writers of the Old Testament made over two thousand direct claims to be speaking the very words of God. Again and again they wrote such phrases as, "The Spirit of the LORD has spoke by me" (2 Sam. 23:2) or "The Word of God came to me" (1 Chr. 17:3). For example, Isaiah opens his prophecy by saying, "Hear, O heavens, and give ear, O earth! For the LORD has spoken" (Is. 1:2). When God speaks, everybody is to listen because He is the final authority.

In the New Testament we find more of the same, especially in the teachings of Jesus. Talking about God's Word in the Sermon on the Mount Jesus said, "Do not think that I came to destroy the Law or the Prophets. I did not come to destroy but to fulfill. For assuredly, I say to you, till heaven and earth pass away, one jot or one tittle will by no means pass from the law till all is fulfilled" (Matt. 5:17, 18).

That even the tiniest part of God's Word has authority is echoed by James when he writes: "For whoever shall keep the whole law, and yet stumble in one point, he is guilty of all" (James 2:10). All of God's Word is authoritative.

But while the Bible claims complete authority over our lives, many people do not always recognize that authority. Today's "all-truth-is-relative" way of thinking takes the Bible off its authoritative pedestal and places it on the shelf as "just another book."

In an article written for *Eternity* magazine, D. Martyn Lloyd-Jones wrote words for the church of the fifties that are especially applicable to the church of today. Lloyd-Jones points out that the attack on Scripture's authority began in the middle of the eighteenth century when scholars began to take a "higher critical" view of Scripture. Naturalistic presuppositions, along with human knowledge and reasoning and new discoveries in science, were all brought to bear in an attempt to analyze the Bible and "get at its real truth." All of this developed into the movement we know as liberalism, which held sway throughout the eighteenth and nineteenth centuries. Liberalism saw the Bible as full of errors, the work of men, and something to be accepted as having no more authority than the works of Shakespeare or Henry Wadsworth Longfellow.

With the dawn of the twentieth century a new movement began. Neo-orthodox thinkers tried to restore some of the Bible's authority by reaffirming the sinfulness of man and claiming that while the Bible is not the Word of God, it "contains the Word of God." As Lloyd-Jones describes it, "The Bible, we are told, is partly the Word of God and partly the word of man. In part it has great authority and in part it has not."[4]

> Lloyd-Jones goes on to point out that this "partly-God's-Word-partly-man's-word" position leads to a view of the Bible which holds part of it in high esteem but then understands other parts of the Bible as full of errors and "utterly useless and valueless."[5]

At that point, observes Lloyd-Jones, we are faced with a basic question:

> Who decides what is true? Who decides what is of value? How can you discriminate and differentiate between the great facts that are true and those that are false? How can you differentiate between facts and teaching? How can you separate the essential message of the Bible from the background in which it is presented? . . . The whole Bible comes to us and offers itself to us in exactly the same way. There is no hint, no suspicion of a suggestion that parts of it are important and parts are not. They all come to us in the same form.[6]

Liberalism and neo-orthodoxy are still with us in every conceivable shape and form. As Lloyd-Jones wrote in 1957:

> The modern position amounts to this, that it is really man's reasons that decide. You and I come to the Bible and we have to make our decisions on the basis of certain standards which are obviously in our minds. We decide that one portion conforms to the message which we believe, and that another does not. We are left still with the position, in spite of all the talk about a new situation today, that man's knowl-

edge and man's understanding are the final arbiter and the final court of appeal.[7]

From ministers and seminary students to lay people in the pews, all of us can get caught up in the doubts and skepticism of our age. Even the greatest of Christian leaders know what it is to wrestle with this. Some have wrestled and lost; others have wrestled and won.

Before he launched his career, Billy Graham struggled with doubts about the Scriptures. Recalling those days, he says:

> I believe it is not possible to understand everything in the Bible intellectually. One day some years ago I decided to accept the Scriptures by faith. There were problems I could not reason through. When I accepted the Bible as the authoritative Word of God—by faith—I found immediately that it became a flame in my hand. That flame began to melt away unbelief in the hearts of many people and to move them to decide for Christ.
>
> The Word became a hammer, breaking up stony hearts and shaping men into the likeness of God. Did not God say, "I will make my words in thy mouth fire" (Jer. 5:14), and "Is not my word like as a fire? saith the Lord; and like a hammer that breaketh the rock in pieces?" (Jer. 23:29)?
>
> I found that I could take a simple outline, then put a number of Scripture quotations under each point; and God would use it mightily to cause men to make a full commitment to Christ. I found that I did not have to rely upon cleverness, oratory, psychological manipulation, apt illustrations, or striking quotations from famous men. I began to rely more and more upon Scripture itself and God blessed it. I am convinced through my travels and experience that people all over the world are hungry to hear the Word of God.[8]

Is the Bible authoritative? Does it need defending? The great preacher, Charles Haddon Spurgeon, said it well: "There is no need for you to defend a lion when he's being attacked. All you need to do is open the gate and let him out."

God's Word Is Effective

One of the most powerful claims to the Bible's infallibility, inerrancy, and authority is its effectiveness. The prophet Isaiah aptly describes the ability of Scripture to get results when he said:

> For as the rain comes down, and the snow from heaven; and do not return there; but water the earth; and make it bring forth and bud; that it may give seed to the sower; and bread to the eater; so shall My word be that goes forth from My mouth; it shall not return to Me void; but it shall accomplish what I please, and it shall prosper in the thing for which I sent it. (Is. 55:10, 11)

One of the best things about being a preacher and a teacher of God's Word is that you know it will do what it says it will do. You are not left worrying about what you will say when your product doesn't work.

There is a story about a lady who lived way out in the country. A vacuum cleaner salesman came by and began to give the woman his high-pressure sales talk.

"Madam, I have the greatest product you have ever seen. This vacuum cleaner will eat up anything. In fact, if I don't control this vacuum, it will suck up your carpet."

Before the woman could reply he went on to say, "Lady, I want to give you a demonstration."

The salesman went to the fireplace, scooped up some ashes and threw them in the middle of the carpet. Then he reached into a bag in his own pocket and poured more dirt and junk right on the carpet. After making a thorough mess he said, "Madam, I want you to watch this product at work. I guarantee it will suck up every bit of everything I've thrown on your rug."

The woman stood there aghast—speechless—and the salesman

went on to say, "Lady, if it doesn't suck up every bit of this, I'll eat it all with a spoon."

The woman looked the salesman in the eye and finally found her voice: "Well, sir, start eating. We ain't got no electricity."

It's tough to be caught in a situation where your product isn't going to work. But that never happens with the Bible. It is always effective, and it always does exactly what it says it will do. Paul talked about this great effectiveness of the Scriptures when he wrote: "For our gospel did not come to you in word only, but also in power, and in the Holy Spirit and in much assurance" (1 Thess. 1:5). When the Word goes forth, it has power. It has the Holy Spirit, and you have the assurance that God's Word will do what it says.

To Sum It Up

So what have we said so far? The Word of God is infallible in its totality, and it is inerrant in all its parts. God's Word is authoritative and demands our obedience. Again and again we see the Bible's infallibility, inerrancy, and authority demonstrated because the Bible is effective. The Bible does what it says it will do.

Everything we have said so far is good, *if* we have one more thing—the presence of the Holy Spirit. The need for this vital extra dimension is well illustrated by a conversation I had with a man on an airplane. As we talked, he continually admitted that he didn't understand the Bible. I didn't really tell him in so many words, but I hinted at why I didn't expect him to understand the Bible. He didn't have the one necessary thing he needed—the life of God in his soul, the presence of the Holy Spirit.

Without the Holy Spirit the Bible is "just another book." When we have the Holy Spirit at work in our hearts, the Bible is *The Book*. We will see why in the next chapter.

Chapter Six

WHO CAN PROVE THAT THE BIBLE IS TRUE?

But how do I know it's true? That question is one of the battle cries of our generation, which is also fond of asking, "Who says I have to do it?" Today it is something of a colossal understatement to say that we live in a world that doesn't respond to authority very well. In fact, just about the whole culture rebels against authority. If you doubt it, ask the police. Ask teachers, coaches, and congressmen. Ask employers, the Supreme Court, and the president.

Deep in the soul of every person is a streak of rugged individualism that begins in the womb and starts to show itself in the cradle. We all want to be our own god. We want to be captains of our soul and masters of our fate. No, we don't respond to authority very well at all.

Is it any wonder then that people question the authority of the Bible? As a minister I can say, "The Bible is the absolute authority for everyone. It is infallible, inerrant, effective, and absolutely authoritative. It is the final word on how we should all live."

The typical response—which can come from Christians as well as non-Christians—is: "How do I *know* that? I'm not going to accept what you say unless you *show* me."

In other words, they want proof. When it comes to the authority of the Scriptures, a lot of people seem to be from Missouri—they have a "show me" attitude. What can you say when someone wants you to prove the Bible is true?

Four Ways to Prove the Bible

If I want to play the "prove-the-Bible-is-true" game I start by speaking from *my personal experience.* I believe the Bible is true because it gives me the experience that it claims it will give me. For example, the Bible says that God will forgive my sins. I believe that. I accepted God's forgiveness, and it happened. How do I know? I have a sense of freedom from guilt.

The Bible also says that if I come to Christ I will be a "new creation." Old things will pass away, and all things will become new. I believed in Christ one day, and it happened just as the Bible said it would. Old things did pass away, and all things did become new. I know, because I experienced it in my own life.

Yes, the Bible really changes lives. Millions of people—from great heads of state to brilliant educators and scientists, from philosophers and writers to generals and historians—could all testify about how the Bible has changed their lives. Millions of people are living proof that the Bible can put lives together and keep them that way.

A stronger argument comes from science. Although the Bible is not a science book, the descriptions referring to scientific processes are accurate.

Take, for example, the hydrological cycle. Rain or snow falls to the ground and runs off into streams, which run into rivers, which run into the sea. Water evaporates from the surface of the ocean and returns to the clouds, where it becomes rain and snow and falls to the ground again. The hydrological cycle is a discovery of modern times, but the Bible speaks of it in Isaiah 55:10: "As the rain comes down, and the snow from heaven; and do not return there; but water the earth" (for similar references, see Job 36:27 and Ps. 135:7).

For another illustration, we can go to the science of geology. Geologists speak of a state called *isostasy,* which can be used to describe the balance of the earth as it orbits through space. Basically the idea behind isostasy is that equal weights are necessary to support equal weights. Land mass must be balanced equally by water mass. In order for the earth to remain stable as it spins in orbit, it must be in perfect balance. But again, the scientists haven't discovered anything that is significantly new or beyond the Bible. The prophet Isaiah also wrote that God "measured the waters in the hollow of His hand" and that He "weighed the mountains in scales; and the hills in a balance" (Is. 40:12).

You can find many other examples of how the Bible matches up with discoveries of modern science.[1] Of course the precise technological language is not there, and for good reason. God wrote the Bible for men of all ages, and while His Word never contradicts science, it also never gets trapped into describing some precise scientific theory that becomes outdated in a few years, decades, or centuries. Long before modern science was born, Augustine gave excellent advice to Christians when he said in effect, "We should not rush headlong to one opinion or the other, because there is always the possibility that a hastily adopted viewpoint can turn out to be false, and if our faith is dependent on that view it can appear false, too. And we will be arguing for our own opinions rather than the real doctrines of Scripture."[2]

A *third significant area that has continued to prove the Bible's accuracy is archaeology*. William F. Albright, recognized throughout the world as a leading Palestinian archaeologist, attests that there is little doubt that archaeology has confirmed the substantial historical accuracy of Old Testament tradition.[3]

For example, higher critics of Scripture doubted the Bible's description of King Solomon's wealth. But archaeologist Henry Breasted, between 1925 and 1934, unearthed the remains of one of Solomon's "chariot cities" at Megiddo in northern Palestine. Breasted found stables capable of holding more than four hundred horses and the remains of barracks for Solomon's chariot battalions which were stationed to guard a strategic trail that ran through Megiddo. Nelson Glueck, another archaeologist, found the remains of a huge refining factory for copper and iron, two metals Solomon used when bartering for gold, silver, and ivory (see 1 Kin. 9:28; 10:22).[4]

Critics of Scripture also doubted the existence of the Hittites, a people the Bible refers to some forty times. Archaeologist Hugh Winckler excavated the Hittite capital of Boghaz-Koi and recovered thousands of Hittite texts, as well as the famous Hittite code.[5]

Other examples of how archaeology confirms the authority of the Bible could fill this book and several dozen others.[6] Archaeology helps us see clearly that our Christian faith rests on facts (actual events) not myths or stories.

Perhaps the strongest objective argument for the validity of Scripture comes from fulfilled Bible prophecy. Peter W. Stoner, a scientist and mathematician, utilized what he called "the principle of probability." This principle holds, that if the chance of one thing happening is one in M and the chance of another thing happening is one in *N*, the chance that they both shall happen is one in $M \times N$. This equation is used in fixing insurance rates. Stoner asked 600 of his students to apply the principle of probability to the biblical prophecy of the destruction of Tyre (see Ezek. 26:3–16), which claims seven definite events: (1) Nebuchadnezzar would take the city; (2) other nations would help fulfill the prophecy; (3) Tyre would be flattened like the top of a rock; (4) the city would become a place where fishermen spread their nets; (5) Tyre's stones and timbers would be laid in the sea; (6) citizens of other cities would become afraid because of Tyre's fall; (7) the old city of Tyre would never be rebuilt. Using the principle of probability in a conservative manner, the students estimated the chances of all seven events occurring as described at one in 400 million, *yet all seven did occur.*

Stoner's students did a similar study on the prophecy that predicted the fall of Babylon (see Is. 13:19). They estimated the chances of the Babylon prophecies occurring at one in 100 billion, but everything stated did come to pass.[7]

Biblical prophecy declares the events of the future with accuracy which is beyond the capability of human wisdom or anticipation. Despite astronomical odds, hundreds of biblical prophecies have come true, and they make the most objective argument for the Bible's authority.

Beyond Arguments and Proofs

While there are many solid arguments for the authority of Scripture, none of them are of much use if someone doesn't want to be convinced. Ultimately this question of the authority of the Scriptures is a matter of faith and not of argument. You may convince a man intellectually of what you're saying, but still he may not of necessity believe in and accept the authority of the Scripture.

Actually there is only one argument that can prove to us that the Bible is true and authoritative for our lives: the work of the Holy Spirit in our hearts and minds. Perhaps no one knew this better than the apostle Paul and there is no clearer description of the work in the heart of the believer in Christ than 1 Corinthians 2:

> And I, brethren, when I came to you, did not come with excellence of speech or of wisdom declaring to you the testimony of God. For I determined not to know anything among you except Jesus Christ and Him crucified. I was with you in weakness, in fear, and in much trembling. And my speech and my preaching were not with persuasive words of human wisdom, but in demonstration of the Spirit and of power, that your faith should not be in the wisdom of men but in the power of God. (1 Cor. 2:1–5)

Paul stressed that he came to the Corinthians with nothing but the simple gospel. The gospel does not need the addition of human philosophy or wisdom. God does not need man's reason, or man's innovation. Everything about the gospel is really very simple. In fact, to the world it sounds so simple it seems foolish. In 1 Corinthians 1:18 Paul writes, "For the message of the cross is foolishness to those who are perishing." And that is exactly what it was to the sophisticated Corinthians, who, like their neighbors in nearby Athens, were always seeking the new theory and the brilliant new philosophy.

In effect the Corinthians were saying, "Paul, you're full of nonsense. Do you expect intellectuals like us, with all of our wisdom and education, to believe that somewhere, sometime one fellow died on a cross and that was the turning point of human history?" People say essentially the same today. "The Bible? That's for little kids and old ladies, isn't it? No intelligent person would believe the Bible. I just can't buy it." I've heard many people say similar things. And Paul agrees with all of them. When it comes to "human wisdom" the Bible certainly does sound like a lot of foolishness.

But Paul isn't preaching human or worldly wisdom. The only people who can know the wisdom that Paul is talking about are Christians. God's wisdom is open only to the minds of believers in Christ as Savior and Lord. Paul then goes on to make two points about true wisdom—how it is discovered and how it is revealed.

True Wisdom Not Humanly Discovered

As I talk with people I hear a lot of opinions about God: "Well, I think God is . . ." "In my opinion, God is . . ." While we all have a right to our own opinions, that can't help us when it comes to knowing God. We can't know God on our own no matter how hard we try. We can't escape the confines of our natural existence, leap into a supernatural dimension, and then come back and tell everyone what we know about God. We can't leave this natural world. We are stuck here, unable to know God on our own.

Christians are always giving testimonies about how "I found the Lord." But the Lord wasn't lost. We were, and He found us. He had to come and find us because we aren't able to transcend our own world. That's why Paul says in 1 Corinthians 2:6 that the wisdom of this age is "coming to nothing." Paul is thinking of the philosophers who keep coming and going, arguing, and changing their views. While philosophy has made contributions down through the ages, there has been a great deal of contradiction and even instability. As one philosophy professor told his class: "Philosophy bakes no bread."

Paul speaks of an entirely different kind of wisdom. He teaches "But we speak the wisdom of God in a mystery, the hidden wisdom which God ordained before the ages for our glory" (1 Cor. 2:7). Before time began, God had a marvelous salvation plan, and He hid it. Then in Christ and in the New Testament, all of these mysteries were revealed.

God had to reveal the mystery, of course, because the brilliant "rulers of this age" didn't understand it. If they had they wouldn't "have crucified the Lord of glory" (1 Cor. 2:8). The rulers of this age Paul was referring to were the Jewish and Roman leaders. They didn't know God, and they didn't know the truth. If they had, they never would have crucified Christ. All the brilliant Romans and all those educated erudite Sadducees and Pharisees, those who were well schooled in the Old Testament, together they all crucified Christ.

Paul then goes on to quote Isaiah, "Eye has not seen, nor ear heard; nor have entered into the heart of man; the things which God has prepared for those who love Him" (1 Cor. 2:9). With all of its quest for truth, the world can't figure out what's going on. There are only two ways you can come to truth, humanly speaking. One is objective, the other is subjective. One uses the experiential empirical method, the other uses reason or logic. When Paul talks about "eye has not seen; nor ear heard," he's talking about the experiential empirical method. But God cannot be observed by our eyes. We can't hear Him or see Him. He does not fit in our test tubes or under our microscopes.

The other way men draw conclusions is through their own reasoning—rationalism. And that's why Paul goes on to say that no mind has conceived what God has prepared. Worldly wisdom can't know God through the study of objective facts, and it can't know Him internally through subjective thought processes. The world is in a hopeless state; but God has a great plan. The secret to knowing God is loving Him through Jesus Christ. The human mind does not discover God. God revealed Himself to the human mind in Christ.

True Wisdom Is Revealed by the Holy Spirit

When I was a student in high school I visited a girl in an iron lung. Fortunately, because polio has been controlled by the Salk vaccine, iron lungs are not in use as much as they once were. It's terrible to see someone in an iron lung—a large casket-like affair with pumps and hoses and dials and gauges—it is not a pleasant sight. This lovely girl had to stay in that iron lung all the time. Anything that came to her had to come from the outside. She wasn't going anywhere.

In a way an iron lung is an apt illustration of the position of natural man. Spiritually speaking, he is in an iron lung of his own capacity. If any wisdom or truth about God is going to come to him, it will have to be brought in from the outside. In his natural state, man isn't going anywhere.

And that is the point Paul is making here in 1 Corinthians 2. The Holy Spirit has invaded man's iron lung with the truth. As the Holy Spirit reveals true wisdom, three elements are discernible: revelation, inspiration, and illumination.

Revelation means the disclosure of something that has been previously hidden, the unveiling of something that has been veiled. The Holy Spirit is the agent who reveals God's wisdom to the Christian as He "searches all things, yes, the deep things of God" (1 Cor. 2:10). No one is better qualified. As Paul points out no one knows the thoughts of a man better than "the spirit of the man which is in him." And "no one knows the things of God except the Spirit of God" (1 Cor. 2:11).

Inspiration is the next step in the process. Inspiration is the method by which the Spirit delivers God's revelation. Paul goes on to say that "we [the apostles] have received, not the spirit of the world, but the Spirit who is from God, that we might know the things that have been freely given to us by God" (1 Cor. 2:13).

Be sure to note that when Paul uses the word "we" he is not referring to all Christians in a general sense. He is referring to the apostles and other writers of Scripture. You and I have received spiritual truth through their writings; but here Paul is talking about his own experience, how he and other apostles received spiritual truths directly from the Spirit.

Paul's reference to how the apostles have received words taught directly by the Spirit matches the teaching in John 14:26 where Jesus tells the disciples, "But the Helper, the Holy Spirit, whom the Father will send in My name, He will teach you all things, and bring to your remembrance all things that I said to you." Jesus' promise is not primarily for all believers for all time. It was spoken to those who would write the New Testament. It was to many of the disciples, later to be called apostles, that God gave power to remember the words of Christ and all that He did. And how did He give that power? It was through inspiration.

When Paul sat down and wrote 1 Corinthians, the Spirit of God took control of him. The Spirit of God breathed into Paul's mind what God wanted said and then Paul used his own vocabulary and his own experience to write Scripture. The Bible is not only God's Word, it is God's *words*.

Revelation and inspiration are only two steps in the work of the Spirit as it is described here in 1 Corinthians 2. Perhaps its most important work is in the third step—*illumination*. Many people have a Bible, but don't really know what's in it. Or they believe in strange and interesting doctrines that are not taught by the Bible at all. The safeguard against misuse of the Bible is the illumination from the Holy Spirit. That is what Paul is talking about when he writes in 1 Corinthians 2:14: "But the natural man does not receive the things of the Spirit of God, for they are foolishness to him; nor can he know them, because they are spiritually discerned."

No matter how religious he might be, the natural man can't understand the real message of Scripture. He can't get out of his iron lung. Not only that, but somebody has pulled his plug! Spiritually speaking, he is dead. In Psalm 119:18, the psalmist prays a beautiful prayer: "Open my eyes, that I may see; wondrous things from Your law." God didn't just give us the law (the Scriptures). He also has to open the eyes of our understanding; and He does this as the Holy Spirit illuminates our minds. Truth is available, but only those who are illuminated will understand it.

The natural man may be able to read God's inspired revelation, but without the illumination of the Holy Spirit it won't make sense to him. Just as a blind man can't see the sun, the natural man can't see the Son of Righteousness. Just as the deaf man can't hear sweet music, the natural man can't appreciate the sweet song of salvation. As Martin Luther said, "Man is like Lot's wife—a pillar of salt. He's like a log or a stone. He's like a lifeless statue that uses neither eyes nor mouth, neither senses nor heart, unless he is enlightened, converted and regenerated by the Holy Spirit."

"He who is spiritual," on the other hand, "judges all things, yet he himself is rightly judged by no one. For 'who has known the mind of the Lord that he may instruct Him?' " (1 Cor. 2:15, 16).

This verse tells us that we have a tremendous and a heavy responsibility. The Holy Spirit is our resident teacher of truth. God's point of reference is within us, and in a spiritual sense we can be judged by no one. The world can laugh at the Christian, mock him, call him a fool, and—in some places in this world still today—can kill him. But no one can judge the spiritual man (the Christian who has the Holy Spirit) because to do that means that person is judging the Lord Himself.

The Christian, however, should not misuse his spiritual status. He must be careful to never think he knows it all because, obviously, there are many natural areas when he does need advice, help, correction, and even judgment. But in the area of the spiritual, Paul says clearly that the Christian is judged by no man.

To Sum It Up

While the Christian can marshal good arguments from personal experience, science, archaeology, and prophecy, he cannot finally "prove" the Bible is true and authoritative. Still, he knows the Bible is true because of his resident truth-teacher—the Holy Spirit. The Holy Spirit is the only one who can prove God's Word is true; and He does this as He works in the heart and mind of the Christian in whom He dwells.

Chapter Seven
What Did Jesus Think of God's Word?

Can you believe in Christ but not in the authority and infallibility of the Bible? You can try, but it will leave you on the horns of a very real dilemma, and here is why: If you say you believe in Christ but doubt the Bible's truthfulness, you are being inconsistent and even irrational. Christ endorsed the Bible as true and authoritative. If you give Christ a place of honor and authority in your life, it follows that to be consistent you have to give Scripture that same honor and authority.

The Deity and Authority of Christ

Despite their lack of understanding at times, the twelve disciples definitely understood that their Master was God in human form and consequently that His word was authoritative. In response to others who decided to forsake Him, Christ asked the Twelve, " 'Do you also want to go away?' But Simon Peter answered Him, 'Lord, to whom shall we go? You have the words of eternal life. Also we have come to believe and know that You are the Christ, the Son of the living God.' " (John 6:67–69).

In the course of John the Baptist's ministry around the Jordan, certain of His followers began to have questions about this prophet: "Now as the people were in expectation, and all reasoned in their hearts about John, whether he was the Christ or not" (Luke 3:15). John, not wishing any misconception of himself to be spread around, gave them an absolute reply:

> I indeed baptize you with water; but One mightier than I is coming, whose sandal strap I am not worthy to loose. He will baptize you with the Holy Spirit and fire. His winnowing fan is in His hand, and He will thoroughly clean out His threshing floor, and gather the wheat into His barn; but the chaff He will burn with unquenchable fire. (Luke 3:16, 17)

John accurately understood his ministry as both prophet and as forerunner to Christ who would possess the authority to decide the eternal destiny of each person.

God the Father directly attested to Christ's authority through two events. One occurred at the baptism of the Lord when a voice out of heaven said of Him, "You are My beloved Son; in You I am well pleased" (Luke 3:22). The other is at the transfiguration where the Father speaks: "This is My beloved Son. Hear Him" (Luke 9:35).

Martyn Lloyd-Jones excellently paraphrases this latter verse:

> In other words, this is the one to listen to. You are waiting for a word. You are waiting for an answer to your questions. You are seeking a solution to your problems. You have been consulting the philosophers; you have been listening; and you have been asking, "Where can we have final authority?" Here is the answer from heaven, from God: "Hear Him." Again, you see, marking Him out, holding Him before us as the last Word, the ultimate Authority, the One to whom we are to submit, to whom we are to listen.[1]

Jesus did not hesitate to assert His unique authority in some very definitive teachings. As part of the "I am" series, Jesus informed His listeners that He was the only bread of life (see John 6:35), the only water of life (see John 4:14; 7:37), the only light of the world (see

John 8:12), the only true shepherd (see John 10:1–18), and the true vine (see John 15:6), and the way, and the truth and the life (John 14:6).

The Sermon on the Mount provides another illustration of the authority with which Jesus spoke. Lloyd-Jones writes:

> We need to remember that it is this characteristic, personal emphasis which brings Him into contrast with the prophets. Those Old Testament prophets were mighty men. They were great personalities entirely apart from their being used by God and anointed by the Holy Spirit. But there is not one of them who ever used this *I*. They all say, "Thus saith the Lord." But the Lord Jesus Christ does not put it like that. He says, "I say unto you." At once He is differentiating between Himself and all others . . . His whole emphasis is upon "these sayings of *mine*." Here is His claim to final authority. And if it is possible to add to such a statement, He did so when He said, "Heaven and earth shall pass away, but *my* words shall not pass away." There is nothing beyond that.[2]

The results were that "the people were astonished at His teaching, for He taught them as one having authority, and not as the scribes" (Matt. 7:28, 29; see Mark 1:22; Luke 4:32). While the multitudes were accustomed to hearing their leaders substantiate their points by referring to past teachers, Jesus relied upon His own authority. The question of the hypocrites in Matthew 21:23 indicates their recognition of His authority. From where did His authority stem? Jesus freely recognized it as coming from God His Father (see Matt. 9:6, 8) who gave Him complete authority: "All authority has been given to Me in heaven and on earth" (Matt. 28:18).

Robert Lightner adequately summarizes the origin of Christ's authority: "The source of such authority is God, and since He was God He could speak thus. The Gospel writers make it very clear that Christ's authority was derived from God, His Father. He had been sent by the Father to do the work of the Father and to declare the words of the

Father. This commission He fulfilled through the power and authority of the Father (John 17:68)."[3]

Did Jesus Doubt the Old Testament?

What did Jesus think of the Scripture of His day, the Old Testament? Did He see it as authoritative? In Matthew 23:35 He apparently defines the Hebrew canon as the books from Genesis (Abel) to post-exilic 2 Chronicles (Zechariah), which encompass the whole Old Testament in terms of Hebrew chronology.

It is also important to note that Jesus never quoted, or alluded, to any apocryphal works. Why was this so? Bible scholar F. F. Bruce explains that the books of the Apocrypha "were not regarded as canonical by the Jews either of Palestine or of Alexandria, and that our Lord and His apostles accepted the Jewish canon and confirmed its authority by the use they made of it, whereas there is no evidence to show that they regarded the apocryphal literature (or as much of it as had appeared in their time) as similarly authoritative."[4]

Although this is admittedly an argument from silence, it is still significant that sixty-four times Jesus quoted or alluded to the Old Testament,[5] while He never referred to other sources. As indicated in chapter four, Christ put His stamp of approval on the Old Testament in several key ways.

Jesus freely acknowledged that all of Scripture pointed to Him. In John 5:39, for example, Jesus said to the Jewish leaders, "You diligently study the Scriptures because you think that by them you possess eternal life. These are the Scriptures that testify about me." Later Jesus explained to the two disciples on their way to Emmaus, "all the Scriptures concerning Himself" (Luke 24:27). To the Eleven He said, "These are the words which I spoke to you while I was still with you, that all things must be fulfilled which were written in the Law of Moses and the Prophets and the Psalms concerning Me" (Luke 24:44).

Christ also said He came to fulfill all Scripture. In Matthew 5:17 He assured the disciples that He did not intend to abolish the Law or the

Prophets but rather to fulfill them. Evidence of this is that Jesus willingly submitted to the Old Testament teachings; and corrected those who accused Him falsely as well (see Mark 2:23–28). Also, Jesus saw Himself as fulfilling the Old Testament prophecies.[6] In Matthew 26:24, He related that He, the Son of Man, would be betrayed "just as it is written about Him" A few verses later Jesus acknowledged to Peter that He could instantly call down twelve legions of angels to protect Himself. This, however, would not have been according to God's plan: "How then could the Scriptures be fulfilled, that it must happen thus?" (Matt. 26:54). In other words, Jesus came to fulfill Scripture. His view of Scripture was that it was about Him, and every detail had to be fulfilled.

Jesus compared the duration of Scripture to the duration of the universe. He said, "It is easier for heaven and earth to pass away than for one tittle of the law to fail"(Luke 16:17). So "all things that are written by the prophets concerning the Son of Man will be accomplished" (Luke 18:31).

Jesus also corroborated the historicity and validity of Old Testament people and events. For example, He confirmed the creation of Adam and Eve by asking, "Have you not read that He who made them at the beginning 'made them male and female,' and said, 'For this reason a man shall leave his father and mother and be joined to his wife, and the two shall become one flesh'?" (Matt. 19:4, 5).

Some have attempted to call the account of the first murder, in which Cain killed Abel, an allegory—fiction that teaches a spiritual truth. But Jesus in a confrontation with the Pharisees, said, ". . . from the blood of Abel to the blood of Zechariah who perished between the altar and the temple. Yes, I say to you, it shall be required of this generation" (Luke 11:51).

On another occasion Jesus made reference to Lot and his wife: "But on the day that Lot went out of Sodom it rained fire and brimstone from heaven and destroyed them all. . . . Remember Lot's wife" (Luke 17:29, 32).

Another Old Testament character whom Jesus saw as historical was Daniel: "When you see the 'abomination of desolation,' spoken of by Daniel the prophet, standing in the holy place (whoever reads, let him understand)" (Matt. 24:15).

Throughout the years some have denied the historical nature of the Flood. But Jesus believed in the Noahic flood. He declared, "But as the days of Noah were, so also will the coming of the Son of Man be. For as in the days before the flood, they were eating and drinking, marrying and giving in marriage, until the day that Noah entered the ark" (Matt. 24:37, 38).

And there are many other facts in the Book of Genesis that He substantiated, such as the call of Moses (see Mark 12:26). In John 6:31, 32, He talked about manna from heaven. In John 3:14, He referred to the brazen serpent lifted up in the wilderness by which Israel was healed. *Over and over again, Jesus agreed to and confirmed the authority of the Old Testament record.*

What About the Theory of Accommodation?

Before concluding our look at Christ's view of Scripture we must settle one other claim made by those who challenge the authority and inerrancy of Scripture. That challenge involves the idea that perhaps Jesus made His teaching fit the beliefs current to His day. Jesus, the argument goes, accommodated His teaching so that He could communicate spiritual truths without alienating the people in Palestine, particularly the religious leaders.

According to biblical scholars Norman Geisler and William Nix:

> Briefly, this theory states that Jesus, in His reference to the Old Testament, accommodates His teaching to the prejudices and erroneous views of His day. It holds that He did not actually mean that Jonah was *really* in the "whale." It claims that Jesus' purpose was not to question the historical truth, nor to establish critical theories, but to preach spiritual and moral values.[7]

Where, in fact, did the accommodation concept originate? John M'Clintock says that the Gnostics were the first ones to hold to this. "They asserted that Christ's doctrine could not be fully known from Scripture alone, because the writer of the New Testament condescended to the stage of culture existing at that time."[8] Later the accommodation theory was propagated by J. S. Sember (1725–1791), the father of German rationalism, and it became a strategic part of liberalism.[9] Accommodation continues to be a favorite argument by liberal and neo-orthodox thinkers of our day who challenge the infallibility and inerrancy of Scripture. But the theory contains several fallacies.

First, the accommodation theory allows for a subjective view of Jesus' teaching. If any part of His words were contaminated by error, then the whole of His message is suspect. Geisler and Nix ask: "If Jesus accommodated so completely and conveniently to current ideas, how can it ever be known with certainty just what He actually believed?"[10] The obvious answer is that no one could know. We could not trust Him, because we could never be sure when He was telling the truth or when He was doing a fast footwork for political or psychological reasons.

Second, perhaps the most serious indictment of this theory is seen in Jesus' dealings with the scribes and Pharisees. If there were any people in His day to whom He might have accommodated His teaching it would have been these religious leaders. But Jesus repeatedly confronted the scribes and Pharisees with the literal teaching of the Old Testament.

One key example is found in Mark 7:6–13 where the traditional teaching of the scribes and Pharisees conflicted with the commandments of God. Accommodation, on the other hand, would call for Jesus to agree with their traditionalistic thinking. In Matthew 22:29, however, Jesus thoroughly rebuked the Sadducees for not knowing the Scripture. In the following chapter Jesus again spoke of the scribes and Pharisees who purport to be followers of Moses, while in reality they hypocritically impose their traditions on others (see Matt. 23:14).

Third, another objection to the accommodation theory involves the character of Jesus. How could He knowingly speak untruth and yet claim to be "the truth" (John 14:6)?[11] If such is the case, His integrity is impugned, and His claim to be Deity is shattered,[12] for the New Testament claims that God cannot lie (see Titus 1:2).

A *fourth objection is related to Christ's use of the Old Testament.* James I. Packer points out that the accommodation theory "assumes that Christ's ideas about the Old Testament are unessential elements in His thought which can be jettisoned without loss to His real message or to His personal authority."[13] In fact, as we previously said, Christ was intimately connected to the Old Testament as He pointed out to the disciples in a post-resurrection appearance: "These are the words which I spoke to you while I was still with you, that all things must be fulfilled which were written in the Law of Moses and the Prophets and the Psalms concerning Me" (Luke 24:44). Earlier on the road to Emmaus, Jesus had explained to Cleopas and his companion "all the Scriptures the things concerning Himself" (Luke 24:27).

The theory of accommodation must be discarded because it does not fit the evidence in the Gospel record. One cannot hold to the theory of accommodation and to the authority of Christ with intellectual honesty. On the other hand, to hold to His authority is to hold to the inerrancy of the Scriptures. The authority and authenticity of Christ and the Scriptures stand or fall together.

To Sum It Up

When examining the testimony of Jesus about the Scriptures, we have to accept one of three possibilities. The first is that there are no errors in the Old Testament, just as Jesus taught. Second, there are errors, but Jesus didn't know about them. Third, there are errors; and Jesus knew about them, but He covered them up.

If the second is true—that the Old Testament contains errors of which Jesus was unaware—then it follows that Jesus was a fallible man, He obviously wasn't God, and we can dismiss the whole thing. If the third alternative is true—that Jesus knew about the errors but covered them up—then He wasn't honest, He wasn't holy, He certainly wasn't God, and again, the entire structure of Christianity washes away like a sand castle at high tide.

I accept the first proposition—that Jesus viewed the Old Testament as the Word of God, authoritative and without error.

The obvious conclusion here is that Jesus accepted the Old Testament authority and passed that same authority on to the New Testament record (see John 14:26; 15:26, 27; 16:12–15).[14] He saw it as the equivalent of His own word. The fulfillment record is as authoritative as the predictive record.

Psalm 119:160 tells us that "the *entirety* of Your word is truth" (italics added). That can only be true if the parts are truth. Based on the authority of Christ, I believe they are. *An authoritative whole demands inerrant parts.*

Reason cannot be allowed to override revelation neither can the authority of Christ be usurped by those He created. Nothing less than the nature of God is at stake.

Chapter Eight

CAN ANYTHING BE ADDED TO THE BIBLE?

In the last few years the renewed interest in the Holy Spirit and use of spiritual gifts has developed an excitement and renewal in many churches. God seems to be revealing Himself and His power in wonderful ways. As we get caught up in all of this, it may be hard to see the difference between what God is saying and doing today and what He said and did in the days when Scripture was being written. Is there a difference between God's Word as given then and the word He is speaking to and through believers today? I think there is a major difference, and it's something we must keep in mind if we are to keep the authority and infallibility of the Bible in proper perspective.

What Did the Writers of Scripture Think?

Suppose you had been one of the writers of a book of the Bible. How would you have viewed your work? Would you have thought you were writing something that came out of your own mind? Or would you have thought it was coming directly from God?

A good way to get answers to these questions is to see what the writers of Scripture had to say for themselves.

As we know, there were some 40 writers of Scripture who produced the Bible over a period of 1,500 years. They lived in separate times and places and had no real opportunity for collaboration to any great degree. But there is one startling characteristic about all of them—from Moses, who wrote the first five books of the Bible, to the apostle John who concluded the New Testament canon with the Book of Revelation. For want of a better term, all of these writers had an air of infallibility. Many of these men were basically simple people without much formal education. Yes, there were a few exceptions who would be called well-educated or sophisticated: Moses was one, Solomon was another. In the New Testament Paul was certainly well-educated as was the physician Luke and James. But the rest were simple farmers, herdsmen, soldiers, and fishermen. Still, all of them—educated or not—wrote with an absolute certainty that what they were writing was the Word of God.

They wrote with absolutely no self-consciousness. They made no disclaimers, no apologies. Instead, they repeatedly and unabashedly claimed to be writing God's Word. One Bible scholar estimates that in the Old Testament alone there are more than 2,600 such claims. If you want to break it down, there are 682 claims in the Pentateuch, 1,307 claims in the prophetic books, 418 claims in the historical books, and 195 claims in the poetic books.[1]

A key example is Moses, who tells God at the burning bush that he cannot possibly go back to Egypt and speak to Pharaoh. God replies: "Who has made man's mouth? Or who makes the mute, the deaf, the seeing, or the blind? Have not I, the LORD? Now therefore, go, and I will be with your mouth and teach you what you shall say" (Ex. 4:11, 12).

The other prophets and writers of Scripture were also certain that what they had to say was something very special. First Samuel 3 records God's visit to the boy Samuel and how He revealed His word to him. First Samuel 3:19 tells us that "the LORD was with [Samuel] and let none of his words fall to the ground."

Jeremiah begins his prophecy by claiming, "The word of the LORD came to me" (Jer. 1:4).

In describing his commissioning by God, Ezekiel recorded that God told him to listen carefully and take to heart all the words that He was speaking. Ezekiel was to go to his countrymen in exile and say, "Thus says the Lord GOD." (Ezek. 3:10, 11).

And no Old Testament prophet makes his calling to speak in a special way any clearer than Amos, who says he was neither a prophet nor a prophet's son, but a shepherd and a keeper of fig trees. "Then the LORD took me as I followed the flock; and the LORD said to me; 'Go, prophesy to My people Israel' " (Amos 7:15).

And what about the New Testament writers? Did they believe as the Old Testament writers did? Did New Testament writers think they were writing the Word of God?

First of all it is interesting to see what the New Testament writers thought about the Old Testament writers. There are at least 320 direct quotes from the Old Testament in the New Testament.[2] New Testament writers refer to the Old Testament some 1,000 times in all. There can be little doubt that the New Testament writers believed that the Old Testament was God's revelation—His inspired Word.

For example, in Romans 15:4 Paul says, "For whatever things were written before were written for our learning, that we through the patience and comfort of the Scriptures might have hope. In Galatians 3:8 Paul is referring to the Old Testament when he writes, "The Scripture, foreseeing that God would justify the Gentiles by faith, preached the gospel to Abraham beforehand, saying, 'In you all the nations shall be blessed.' "

But do any New Testament writers ever claim other New Testament writers are inspired? As noted in chapter four, 2 Peter 3:14–16 Peter refers to "our beloved brother Paul, [who] according to the wisdom given to him, has written to you, as also in all his epistles, speaking in them of these things, in which are some things hard to understand, which untaught and unstable people twist to their own destruction, *as they do also the rest of the Scriptures*" (italics added). What was Peter saying? Two things: Paul wrote in a certain way in all of his letters, and what he wrote is Scripture. Peter was saying that Paul's epistles are inspired—the Word of God.

Paul often claims to be communicating inspired revelation, given to Him directly from God. For example, in Galatians 1:11, "But I make known to you, brethren, that the gospel which was preached by me is not according to man. For I neither received it from man, nor was I taught it, but it came through the revelation of Jesus Christ."

One other good example of Paul's claims to inspiration is

1 Thessalonians 2:13: "We also thank God without ceasing, because when you received the word of God which you heard from us, you welcomed it not as the word of men, but as it is in truth, the word of God, which also effectively works in you who believe." Paul couldn't have said it any more plainly than that. He believed that he taught and wrote God's very word. Either Paul had a monumental ego or he was telling the truth.

From the beginning of the Bible to the very end, its writers were fully convinced that they were speaking the true words of God. Their work bears a mark of inspiration and authority that is unshared by any other writings before or since.

The Canon Is Closed—for Good

Coming back to the question that opened this chapter, is there a distinct difference between how God spoke long ago through prophets and apostles and how He is speaking today? Without question, God is doing some wonderful things in our own day. Through His Holy Spirit He is in the business of guiding and empowering His children to witness, write, speak, and act with extraordinary spiritual impact and power. However, He is not in the business of inspiring (breathing out) any more scriptural revelation. The canon is closed.

That word "canon" may need some definition and explaining. Mention the canon of Scripture in a group of believers and you often get puzzled looks. They know God's Word is called a two-edged sword (see Heb. 4:12) but they can't seem to recall the passage that compares it to firearms. (Some people may be wondering if God's "canon" is a 12-inch or a 16-inch model.)

Actually, the word "canon" is a metaphor, a play on words. It comes from the Greek word *kanon*, meaning "a rod or bar," "a measuring rule, standard, or limit."[3] This Greek term *kanon* originally came from a root word that meant "a reed." In Bible times a reed was used as a Hebrew unit of measure. So, the word came to mean, in a metaphorical sense, a measuring rod, or standard.

The term was used in many ways: in grammar, as a rule of procedure; in chronology, as a table of dates; in literature, as a list of books or works that would correctly be attributed to a given author.[4] Eventually, the term canon was used to refer to the completed list of books given to man by God. Athanasius, bishop of Alexandria, referred to the completed New Testament in A.D. 350 as the canon.[5] In other words, he labeled the collection of 27 books used in the New Testament churches as the final part of God's revelation, which had started with the Old Testament books.

Although some of the books in the New Testament canon were challenged, the final choice of Athanasius and other early church fathers held up. Today, when we use the term "canon of Scripture" we are actually saying the Bible is complete. God has given us His revelation. The Bible is our standard—efficient, sufficient, infallible, inerrant, and authoritative. As God's standard, it is binding and determinative in evaluating any other writing, concept, or idea.

How the Canon Was Chosen

To know what the word "canon" means is helpful, but we are still left with a key question: How did the church fathers decide which books belonged in the canon?

Although the word "canon" wasn't used to refer to the Scriptures in Old Testament times, there was still a clear concept that the Old Testament books were a unified set of sacred writings that was unique.

Two basic tests were used to determine whether a book belonged in the Old Testament canon: (1) Was it inspired by God, written by a prophet or someone with the gift of prophecy? (2) Was it accepted, preserved, and read by God's people, the Israelites?

Some writers of Old Testament Scripture were not known officially as prophets. For example, Daniel was actually a Jew who had risen to the rank of a high government official while being held in captivity in Babylon. David and Solomon were two of the most famous Hebrew kings. Ezra was a scribe. Nehemiah was the cupbearer to King Artaxerxes while in captivity in Babylon and later became governor of the restored city of Jerusalem. Still, all of these men were considered to have prophetic powers or gifts. They were used by God to write and speak for Him.

The Old Testament canon was closed (that is, the last book was written and chosen) around 425 B.C. with the prophecy of Malachi. There was no question which books were inspired by God. In the first place, the writers claimed to be inspired (discussed earlier in this chapter); and when the people of God checked their writings, they found no errors. They fit history, geography, theology—everything they knew that would have a bearing on determining inspiration.

Jewish tradition holds that the final compilers of the Old Testament canon were part of the Great Synagogue, that school of scribes founded by Ezra after the Jews returned from captivity in Babylon. Interestingly enough there were many attempts to add to the Scriptures back then, just as there are today. Efforts were made to add some fourteen non-canonical books to the Old Testament. This collection, called the Apocrypha, included 1 and 2 Esdras, Tobit, Judith, The Best of Esther, The Wisdom of Solomon, Ecclesiasticus, Baruch (with the epistle of Jeremiah), The Song of the Three Holy Children, The History of Susanna, Bell and the Dragon, The Prayer of Manasses, and 1 and 2 Maccabees.

The apocryphal books were not allowed into the Old Testament canon by the Jews, however, because: (1) They were written long after the canon was completed, about 400 B.C., and lacked the prophetic quality to stamp them as inspired Scripture.[6] (2) None of the apocryphal writers claim divine inspiration, and some openly disclaim it. (3) Apocryphal books contain errors of fact and teach questionable ethics and doctrines. For example, apocryphal writings justify suicide and assassination and also teach praying for the dead.

Interestingly enough, the Roman Catholic Church accepted the apocryphal books, and they were included as part of the Roman Catholic versions of the Bible.

How the New Testament Books Were Chosen

Tests used by the early Christian church to determine New Testament Scripture were somewhat the same as those used for the Old Testament books.

Was the book authored by an apostle or someone closely associated with an apostle? Again, the key question was the book's inspiration. And to be inspired it had to be written by an apostle, someone who had walked and talked with the Lord or someone who had been a close companion of an apostle. For example, Mark was not an apostle, but he was a close associate of Peter. Luke, the only Gentile writer of the New Testament, was not an apostle but he worked closely with Paul who was an apostle through his special experience on the Damascus Road.

Jesus had promised the apostles the power to write inspired Scripture when He told them in the Upper Room: "But the Helper, the Holy Spirit, whom the Father will send in My name, He will teach you all things, and bring to your remembrance all things that I said to you" (John 14:26). This promise by the Lord is primarily to His apostles, not to Christians today. And the apostles knew it. As we saw earlier in the chapter they claimed inspiration for themselves or confirmed it in the writings of their fellow apostles. Without question, the key test of Scripture was apostolic authority.

Another test applied by the early church was content. Did the writing square with apostolic doctrine? In those early years of the church, heretics such as the Gnostics would try to slip in a phony book, but none ever made it. If it didn't square with apostolic doctrine, it didn't pass. The doctrinal aberrations were too easy to spot.

A third test asked if the book was read and used in the churches. Did the people of God accept it, read it during worship, and make its teachings part of daily living?

And the final test determined whether the book was recognized and used by the next generations after the early church, especially by the apostolic fathers. Church leaders, such as Polycarp, Justin Martyr, Tertullian, Origen, Eusebius, Athanasius, Jerome, and Augustine, used and approved the apostolic writings. It is important to note, however, that the church leaders did not force certain books on the church. No one man or group of men made a certain book canonical. God determined the canon; man discovered it through long and steady usage. The canon finally emerged through the combined conviction of church leaders and church members working in harmony and guided by the Holy Spirit.

As with the Old Testament, a formidable group of apocryphal New Testament books also sprang up. These included the Epistle of Barnabus, the Apocalypse of Peter, the Gospel of Nicodemus, and the Shepherd of Hermas. There were also "Gospels" of Andrew, Bartholomew, Thomas, and Phillip. But all these failed to make the final New Testament canon because they failed one or more of the key tests of authenticity.

The canonical determination and collection of genuine and inspired books continued slowly and gradually. No church council ever decreed an "official" New Testament canon, but several councils did recognize the consensus of the people and the existence of canonical books. By the end of the fourth century the collection was complete. The canon was closed.[7]

What Happens When You Add "More Revelation"?

The false apocryphal books of the Old and New Testaments (also called the *pseudepigrapha*) were only the first attempts to add "other revelation" to Scripture.[8] Down through the centuries, and into our present day, different individuals and groups have claimed their works and writings are equal to the Bible in authority and inspiration. And always, the result has been error and spiritual chaos. For examples, you need look no further than the claims made by major cults.

The Mormons have put three such works on par with the Scripture: *Doctrine and Covenants*, *Pearl of Great Price*, and the *Book of Mormon*. For example, the Book of Alma (5:45, 46) states: "Do ye not suppose that I know of these things myself? Behold, I testify unto you that I do know that these things whereof I have spoken are true. And how do ye suppose that I know of their surety? Behold, I say unto you they are made known unto me by the Holy Spirit of God . . . and this is the spirit of revelation which is in me."[9]

The Christian Scientists have elevated *Science and Health with Key to the Scriptures* to a scriptural level. One of their documents states that "because it is not a human philosophy, but a divine revelation, the divinity-based reason and logic of Christian Science necessarily separates it from all other systems."[10] Mary Baker Eddy, called "the revelator of truth for this age,"[11] wrote that "I would blush to think of *Science and Health with Key to the Scriptures* as I have were it of human origin and were I apart from God its author. I was only a scribe."[12]

The Jehovah's Witnesses commit the same error when they say of their publication, "*The Watchtower* is a magazine without equal on earth, because God is the author."[13]

Another illustration of someone thinking he has new revelation is David Berg, leader of the Children of God. Also referring to himself as Moses, a latter-day prophet, and David, King of Israel, Berg wrote some five hundred letters in five years. According to a report in *Christianity Today*, "Berg, who is said to have several concubines, insists that his letters are 'God's Word for today' and have supplanted the biblical Scriptures (God's Word for yesterday)."[14]

The preceding are only a few examples, but they illustrate a vital point that is as true today as it was when the canon was being chosen: whoever criticizes, questions, challenges, subtracts from or adds to the authoritative Word of God is ultimately undermining the divine authority of the Lord Jesus Christ and putting man—the creature—in a place of authority instead.

To Sum It Up

The writers of Scripture spoke with special conviction and authority that could come only from God. They did not use phrases like, "I think I am right" or "You probably won't agree with me, but . . ."

Instead they said again and again in different ways: "Thus says the Lord" and "God has put His words in my mouth." They did not guess their writings were inspired; they *knew* it.

The "canon of Scripture" is a term all Christians should know and understand better. It includes the sixty-six books that have been determined to be the infallible rule of faith and practice for the church for all time. Since the close of the New Testament canon in the fourth century, some people have wondered if we shouldn't be able to add to the canon. After all, God has continued to act and speak since those first centuries through the Holy Spirit of Christ. But Revelation 22:18 clearly states: "For I testify to everyone who hears the words of the prophecy of this book: If anyone adds to these things, God will add to him the plagues that are written in this book." Of course you can scoff and say this warning applies only to the Book of Revelation, not the entire Bible. But before you congratulate yourself too loudly, realize that the Book of Revelation is the last book of the Bible, by its very nature, by its content, and by choice of those who determined the canon. If you add to Revelation, you add to the Bible, and put yourself in danger of the curse in Revelation 22:18.

Admittedly, literal plagues have not necessarily come upon some of those who have added to Scripture. (In other cases, their fates have been sad and even terrible.) God may be withholding the force of the curse in Revelation 22:18 until Judgment Day. But one thing is clear: To allow anyone, or everyone, to claim to speak revelation from God is to pay too high a price. Christ has put His own stamp of authority on Scripture. The church has discovered the canon of God's Word under the guidance of the Holy Spirit. To abandon, or even downplay in the slightest way, the uniqueness of Scripture as the only truly inspired Word of God is to invite a spiritual free-for-all.

Chapter Nine
HOW DOES GOD'S WORD CHANGE US?

The Bible is an amazing book. It's amazing in that it stands up to many tests of authenticity. But beyond that, it's particularly amazing when looked at from a spiritual and moral perspective.

The Bible claims to be alive and powerful. That's a tremendous statement. No other living book *exists*. There are some books that change your thinking, but this is the only book that can change your nature. This is the only book that can totally transform you from the inside out.

There's a section in Psalm 19 that is Scripture's own testimony to itself. This is what it says:

> The law of the LORD is perfect, converting the soul; The testimony of the LORD is sure, making wise the simple; The statutes of the LORD are right, rejoicing the heart; The commandment of the LORD is pure, enlightening the eyes; The fear of the LORD is clean, enduring forever; The judgments of the LORD are true and righteous altogether. (Ps. 19:7–9)

Let's look at each aspect separately.

The Bible Is Perfect

First, "the law of the LORD" is a Hebrew term used to define Scripture. Psalm 19 specifies that it is "perfect"—a comprehensive treatment of truth that is able to transform the soul. The Hebrew word translated soul (*nepesh*) refers to the total person. It means the real you—not your body but what is inside. So the truths in Scripture can totally transform a person.

You may say, "I'm not interested in being transformed." Then you probably aren't interested in the Bible. The Bible is for people who have some sense of desperation about where they are. It is for people who don't have the purpose in their lives they wish they had. They're not sure where they are, where they came from, or where they're going. There are things in their lives they wish they could change. They wish they weren't driven by passions they can't control. They wish they weren't victims of circumstance. They wish they didn't have so much pain in life. They wish their relationships were all they ought to be. They wish they could think more clearly about things that matter in their lives. That's who this book is for: people who don't have all the answers and who want something better.

The Bible says that the key to this transformation is the Lord Jesus Christ. God came into the world in the form of Christ. He died on a cross to pay the penalty for your sins and mine and rose again to conquer death. He now lives and comes into the lives of those who acknowledge Him as their Lord and Savior, transforming them into the people God means for them to be. If you're content with the way you are, you're not going to look to the Word of God for a way to change. But if you're aware of your guilt, if you want to get rid of your anxiety and the patterns of life that desperately need to be changed, if you have some emptiness in your heart, if there's some longing that has never been satisfied, and if there are some answers you just can't seem to find, then you're just the person to look into the Word of God to determine if in fact it can do what it says it can. Millions are living proof that it can. It can transform you completely through the power of Christ, the One who died and rose again for you.

The Bible Is Sure

Second, Psalm 19 says that the Scripture is "sure"—absolute, trustworthy, reliable—"making wise the simple." The Hebrew word translated "simple" comes from a root that speaks of an open door. Ancient Jewish people described a person with a simple mind as someone with a head like an open door: everything comes in; everything goes out. He doesn't know what to keep out and what to keep in. He's indiscriminate, totally naive, and unable to evaluate truth. He doesn't have any standards by which to make a judgment.

The Bible says it is able to make such a person wise. Wisdom to the Jew was the skill of daily living. To the Greek it was sheer sophistry—an abstraction. So when the Hebrew text says it can make a simple person wise, it means it can take the uninitiated, naive, uninstructed person who's undiscerning and unskilled and make him skilled in every aspect of daily living. What a fantastic promise!

The Bible touches every area of life. You want to know about relationships? It touches that. You want to know about marriage? It touches that. You want to know about a work ethic? It touches that. You want to know about the factors of the human mind? You want to know about motive? You want to know why you do what you do and how to do it better? You want to know how to get the most out of your life? You want to know what you're to live for? It's all there. The matters of skill in daily living are all there. It tells you about attitudes, reactions, responses, how to treat people, how you're to be treated by people, how to cultivate virtue in your life—every aspect of living is covered in the pages of the Bible. References tools, such as the *MacArthur Study Bible* and topical analyses of the Bible, can easily point you to verses on various subjects. With all of its power and wisdom, the Bible can take a person with no understanding and make him skilled in the matter of daily living.

You may ask, "How does that happen?" It happens not just by reading the book but by committing your life to Jesus Christ, the Subject and the Author of the book. He comes to live in you and applies the truth of the Word to your life.

Third, the Bible is right. The Word of God—called "the precepts of the Lord"—is right. In Hebrew, that means it sets out a right path or lays out a right track. And the result is joy to the heart.

I look back at times in my own life when I didn't know what direction to go, what my future was, or what my career ought to be. Then I began to study God's Word to submit myself to God's Spirit, and, all of a sudden, God laid out the path for me. It's been fantastic to see how Scripture lays out that path. And as I walk in that path, I experience joy, happiness, and blessing. In fact, I find so much satisfaction in life that people sometimes believe something's wrong with me. Even difficulty brings satisfaction, because it creates a way in which God can show Himself faithful. Even unhappiness can be a source of happiness. In John 16 Jesus compares the disciples' sorrow at His leaving to the pain of a woman having a baby. There's joy in that kind of pain which yields such a joyous result.

I know you want a happy life. I know you want peace, joy, meaning, and purpose. I know you want the fullness of life that everybody seeks. The Bible says, "[Happy] are those who hear the word of God and keep it" (Luke 11:28). Why? Because God blesses their faithfulness and obedience. You can have a happy life without sin, without sex outside of marriage, without drugs, and without alcohol. God is not a cosmic killjoy. I know some people who believe He is. They think God runs around saying, "There's one having fun; get him!" They believe God wants to rain on everybody's parade. But that isn't so. God made you. He knows how you operate best. And He knows what makes you happy. The happiness He gives doesn't stop when the party's over. It lasts because it comes from deep within.

The Bible Is Pure

Fourth, the psalmist says the Word of God is "pure [lucid], enlightening the eyes." The simplest Christian understands things that many scholarly people don't know. Because I know the Bible, things are clear to me that aren't clear to others.

The autobiography of English philosopher Bertrand Russell, written near the end of his life, implies that philosophy was something of a washout to him. That's shocking. He spent his life musing on reality but was not able to get anywhere. I don't believe I'm Russell's equal intellectually, but I do know the Word of God. Scripture enlightens the eyes, particularly concerning the dark things of life. What about death? What about disease? What about sad tragic things? What about the devastation of the world? Don't you get sick of picking up the paper and reading about lying, cheating, murder, and war? Scripture deals with the tough issues of life.

I can go to a Christian who is facing death and see joy in his heart. My grandmother died when she was ninety-three years old. She was lying in bed, and the nurse told her it was time to get up. My grandmother said, "No, I'm not getting up today." When the nurse asked why, my grandmother said, "I love Jesus, and I'm going to heaven today, so don't bother me." Then she smiled and did.

Do you have that kind of hope?

When I was a boy I used to go to Christ Church in Philadelphia and read epitaphs written about Americans who have had a great impact on our country. Benjamin Franklin wrote his own epitaph:

The body of
Benjamin Franklin, printer,
(Like the cover of an old book,
Its contents worn out
And stript of its lettering and gilding)
Lies here, food for worms!
Yet the work itself shall not be lost,
For it will, as he believed, appear once more
In a new
And more beautiful edition,
Corrected and amended
By its Author!

Do you have that hope? Do you understand the dark things? Can you look death in the eye and say, "This is not the end; it is but the beginning for me"? What can you say to someone who loses a child?

What can you say to someone who loses a spouse to cancer or heart disease? Are you roaming around in the confusion in which many people find themselves? Where do you go for the dark things to be made clear?

I go to the Word of God, and I find clarity there.

The Bible Is Clean

Further, Psalm 19:9 says that the Word of God is "clean, enduring forever."

The only things that last forever are things untouched by the devastation of evil—another word for sin. The word of God is clean. It describes and uncovers sin, but it is untouched by evil. And even though it is an ancient document, every person in every situation in every society that's ever existed can find in this book things that endure forever. Here's a book that never needs another edition. It never needs to be edited, never has to be updated, never out of date or obsolete. It speaks to us as pointedly and directly as it ever has to any one in any century since it was written. It's so pure that it lasts forever.

When I was in college I studied philosophy. Almost every philosophy I studied was long dead. In the liberal arts area I studied psychology. In graduate school I took more psychology. Almost every form of psychotherapy that I read about is now obsolete or has been replaced by more progressive thinking.

But there's one thing that never changes, and that is the eternal Word of God. It is always relevant.

The Bible Is True

Finally, and most pointedly, Psalm 19:9 says that the Word of God is "true." Do you know how hard it is to find something that's true today? Are newspapers true? Are magazines true? Are politicians, doctors, and lawyers generally truthful? Nowadays, it seems there's no premium on truth.

Do you know why people find it so easy to lie? Because they're fed up with trying to find truth. Pilate, when he sent Jesus to the cross, said, "What is truth?" (John 18:38). The context makes clear that he was being cynical.

I remember meeting a young man on drugs who was living in an overturned refrigerator box by a stream in the mountains of northern California. I was hiking through the area and asked if I could introduce myself. We talked a little while. It turned out he was a graduate of Boston University. He said, "I've escaped." I asked, "Have you found the answers?" "No," he said, "but at least I've gotten myself into a situation where I don't ask the questions." That's the despair of not knowing the truth.

People look for truth. Do you realize how much written information is available today? I remember reading that tens of thousands of pages of material are printed every sixty seconds in our society today. I called the Los Angeles Public Library and asked how many volumes were there, and the number they gave was absolutely mind-boggling. In fact, we now have so much information that we can't store it in books anymore. Scientists are developing laser technology and molecular storage technology that will eventually make it possible to store the entire Library of Congress on an object the size of a sugar cube!

Scripture describes some people as "always learning and never able to come to the knowledge of the truth" (2 Tim. 3:7). I'm not talking about mathematical truth; I'm talking about the truth of life, death, God, man, sin, right, wrong, heaven, hell, hope, joy, and peace. People can't find it on their own.

Chapter Ten

HOW DOES GOD'S WORD MAKE US FREE?

What is truth? Pilate asked Jesus that question, and people are still asking Him the same question today. As I talk with one person or another about the truth to be found in Jesus Christ, they reply, "Well, I don't quite know what the truth is." Some even claim to have stopped looking. One man told me, "I used to hassle myself about whether or not I'd really ever know everything and get it all figured out, and I just finally decided to set it aside and forget it. I don't need that grief. So I just don't bother to worry about it."

Granted, "knowing *everything*" and "getting it *all* figured out" is enough to discourage anyone. In today's society tens of thousands of new pages of material are printed every sixty seconds. We are cranking out literally tons of information. Books can no longer contain it all without becoming too big and cumbersome; so we have begun to use microfilm, microfiche, and compact disc storage.

No doubt about it, we have a lot of information, a lot of knowledge, but we are still not sure about the truth. The Bible mentions people who are "always learning but never able to acknowledge the truth" (2 Tim. 3:7).

For a lot of people, life is like that. They read and study and think and talk and listen, but they never find the truth. They never settle on anything. The frustration becomes overwhelming.

One time I was talking to a group of about ten young people who had dropped out of society to live in a woodsy campsite commune. They started giving me their philosophy of life, so I asked the ultimate question: "What is truth?" They all looked at each other, almost stunned. Then a fellow stepped out of the group and said, "Yin Yang."

"Yin Yang?"

"Yeah, man, Yin Yang is where it's at."

"What's Yin Yang?" I wanted to know.

"You don't know what Yin Yang is? How can you live without Yin Yang? Here, I'll show you."

So he took a stick and drew an oblong circle on the ground. Then he drew a curved line through the middle of the oblong circle and made two equal parts. Next he drew two circles of equal size in each part of the original oblong circle. This gave him two sets, or opposites. Then he said: "See it? That's Yin Yang, man. Groove on that."

"What does it do?" I wanted to know.

"Don't you get it?" he said. "Don't you know that if there wasn't black, there wouldn't be a white? If there wasn't an up, there wouldn't be a down? If there wasn't an out, you wouldn't understand what an in was?"

After he went through a string of opposites, I asked, "So what does that do for me?"

"That's where it's at, man. That's Yin Yang. Life is opposites."

I said, "You mean you've lived all your life and only discovered Yin Yang, and that's it?" All he had to hang on to was Yin Yang. The only truth he had found was the elemental concept of opposites!

My commune friend may be an extreme example, but he illustrates the plight of a lot of people. Their souls long for truth, but they remain in the chains of doubt, indecision, never quite knowing—or Yin Yang.

What God's Word Says about Truth and Freedom

The best place to go to find just where and how the Bible is the source of truth and freedom is to the words of Truth Himself: Jesus Christ. In John 8, Jesus was in one of several heated arguments with Jews who were challenging His teachings. Some of these people, however, were beginning to believe, at least a little bit, and "even as he spoke, many put their faith in him" (John 8:30). All this sounds encouraging until we take a closer look. Most biblical commentators believe that at this point these people could be called "half converts." Their faith was not enough to set them free from sin, not enough to save them."[1]

They were beginning to believe that Jesus is who He claims to be: the Messiah. Jesus wanted to take them from their half-faith to full faith and full salvation. He wanted to take them all the way to real truth and real liberty. In the next few verses (John 8:31–37), we can hear Him talk about three concepts: the progress of freedom, the pretense of freedom, and the promise of freedom.

The Progress of Freedom

How does anyone make progress toward real freedom? In John 8:31, 32, Jesus spells it out: "If you abide in My word, you are My disciples indeed. And you shall know the truth, and the truth shall make you free." This is how to progress toward freedom. First you believe, then you hold tight to Christ's teaching. Holding on to His teaching—"continuing in His Word" as other versions translate it—is evidence of true faith.

Why did Jesus say this to the crowd? Because He recognized their half-faith condition. The same thing happened in the second chapter of John. Jesus had just finished cleansing the Temple of money changers, and John observed that "many believed in His name when they saw the signs which He did" (John 2:23). Did Jesus celebrate or say "Amen"? Hardly. "But Jesus did not commit Himself to them, because he knew all men. . . . He knew what was in man" (John 2:24, 25).

Jesus knew that their faith was not saving faith. They believed what they had seen Him do, but there was no commitment.

You can find the same problem in several other scenes in Scripture. When Jesus teaches the parable of the sower He talks about seed falling on rocky soil. This represents people who believe but have no real root, no commitment. When temptation or trial comes, they fall away (see Luke 8:11–15). In John 12:42–44 you can read about Jewish leaders who believed in Jesus, "but because of the Pharisees they did not confess Him, lest they should be put out of the synagogue; for they loved the praise of men more than the praise of God." They believed, but they would not confess. They were caught in the middle, believing partially but not completely—in a state of half-faith.

The point of all these examples is that "believing" in Christ is not enough, James tells us that "even the demons believe . . . and tremble" (James 2:19). I have talked to a certain man for years about Christ and salvation. His answer? "I believe everything, but I am not ready to give Him my life." That says it all. There must be belief, but there must also be confession—commitment.

And that is why Jesus tells this crowd of Jews, "If you abide in My word, you are My disciples indeed" (John 8:31). James tells us, "faith by itself, if it does not have works, is dead" (see James 2:17). Jesus is saying the same thing. He is saying, "Show me the character of your faith by continuing in my Word—by doing what I say and living as I live." The word *abide* implies obedience. The true disciple *abides, continues,* and *obeys* the living Word of the living Christ.

Many Christians make a false dichotomy out of receiving Jesus as Savior and Lord. They will say, "Three years ago I accepted Christ as Savior, but tonight I want to make Him Lord." Their motive for making such a statement is excellent, but they are a bit mistaken. We don't *make* Christ Lord; He already is. When you receive Him as Savior, He becomes Lord as well. The question is not, "Is Christ Lord of my life?" The question is, "Do I obey Christ's Lordship?"

There are people who claim to be Christ's disciples, but they have little love for His Word, for the truth. A true disciple is oriented to the Word of God. People say to me, "Why do you just teach the Bible?" What else am I supposed to do? Where else are Christians to find and learn the truth?

The word *disciple* means, literally, a learner. A true disciple loves to learn at the feet of Jesus. And then he or she gets up, goes out, and gets involved, A true disciple is not just a hearer, but a doer as well (see James 1:22). When we sit at the feet of Jesus, we shall know the truth and we shall be able to *do* the truth. Why? *Because He is the truth.*

But there is even more. In John 14:26 Jesus tells His disciples: "But the Counselor, the Holy Spirit, whom the Father will send in my name, will teach you all things." True, this promise was primarily for the disciples themselves. As we saw earlier, the Holy Spirit did come to guide and empower them as they wrote inspired Scripture. But Jesus' promise of the Holy Spirit extends to every believer in every age. God plants the Holy Spirit in your life, and then He guides you into more and more truth.

But that's not all. God also provides the textbook for learning truth. In John 17:17 Jesus prayed for His disciples and said: "Sanctify them by the truth; your word is truth." And where is God's Word? It's in the Scriptures.

So we have Christ, Truth incarnate. We have the Holy Spirit, our Counselor and Guide (not a drill sergeant). And we have the textbook, the Bible, God's inspired, infallible Word. It all adds up to the truth and once we discover the truth, says Jesus in John 8:32, we are free. Free from what? Free from the chains of spiritual death; free from the prison of sin; free from Satan's binding power; free from the search for truth; free from the frustrations of having to settle for nihilism, dropping out, or Yin Yang.

The Pretense of Freedom

Coming back to the scene in John 8, we note that the Jews listening to Jesus didn't respond too positively. Instead of accepting His offer they built a wall of self-righteousness. In John 8:33, we hear them saying that they are descendants of none other than Abraham. They had never been slaves to anyone. How could Jesus say that they shall be set free? Who needs it? As for never being slaves, these people seem to have short memories. At that moment, they were in bondage to Rome. Before that, it was the Syrians and the Greeks. Before that, it was the Babylonians and before that it was the Egyptians. Every time they celebrated the Passover they were remembering release from a time of slavery.

But let's give them the benefit of the doubt and assume they are not talking about political freedom, but instead the freedom of their spirits, their souls. Perhaps they were saying, "In our hearts we are free because we are God's chosen ones." Here they are on ground that is a little better, but still very shaky. They were trying to get to heaven on Abraham's coattails. They thought God will accept and bless them because of their racial descent. They were so sure they were saved through Abraham that they threw up a wall Jesus couldn't penetrate. He offered them freedom, but they didn't need it or Him.

These stubborn Jews illustrate perfectly a basic scriptural principle. You can't give someone a drink unless there is thirst; you can't give someone food unless there is hunger; you can't give someone freedom unless there is an awareness of slavery.

But Jesus didn't give up. He got right to the point: "Most assuredly, I say to you, whoever commits sin is a slave of sin" (John 8:34).

Jesus cut right through their hypocrisy and sham. He confronted the Jews with their sin; and they all knew they had plenty of that. In fact in this verse, John uses the Greek word *doulos* which means bond slave—someone in the most base kind of slavery. Jesus said, in effect, "You think you are free, but you are the most slavish of the slaves."

The Promise of Freedom

But Jesus doesn't leave His Jewish listeners in bondage. First, He gives them a warning by saying, "And a slave does not abide in the house forever, but a son abides forever" (John 8:35). In this translation the word "son," has a small *s*, which is correct. Jesus isn't referring to Himself, but to sons in general, those who have permanent rights in their homes while slaves have none. Slaves can be cast out of a home at any time.

Why did Jesus tell these Jews this? Because the Old Testament era was ending. Their Abrahamic security had faded. Unbelieving Jews were just as condemned to spiritual slavery as unbelieving Gentiles. So, what could they do? How could they become sons, not slaves?

Jesus went right on: "Therefore if the Son makes you free, you shall be free indeed" (John 8:36).

The only one who can free a slave is a rightful heir, a person who has a place in the family. Only the father or the son can release the slaves. The same is true on a spiritual plane. If Christ, the Son, sets you free, you are free indeed. Whoever believes in and continues to follow the Son, is a son of God himself (see John 1:12).

In a few brief sentences Jesus offers the crowd of hostile Jews real truth and real freedom. Do they accept? You can read about the outcome in the rest of John 8, but Jesus says it all in v. 37. They—the Jews—are Abraham's descendants. They have a wonderful heritage of God's guidance, truth, and faith, but Jesus observes: "But you seek to kill Me, because My word has no place in you." Before the scene is played out the crowd picks up stones to stone Jesus, but He slips away. They turn from the truth and choose slavery rather than freedom.

How Free Am I?

About now you may be saying, "All this is interesting, but I'm a bit farther down the road than that. I have admitted my need. I am no slave of sin, I'm a son of God and know it. Can the Bible be a further source of truth and freedom for me, or do I already have all it has to offer?"

Or perhaps you are having a few gnawing doubts. It says right there in John 8 that the Son shall make you free indeed, but you don't always feel that free. Why not? The answer is back in John 8:31: If you hold to Christ's teaching you are really His disciple. If you continue in His Word, you are a true student at His feet; and He has a great deal to teach you.

Throughout history every generation has probably thought it was living in the most challenging, difficult time that could be experienced. We are no exception; and we have good reason to be concerned. Technology is running amuck. We have the finest, the best, the greatest, the biggest, and the most, but we are in big trouble. The miracle of the motion picture has produced porno flicks. The miracle of television and the computer has brought a growing flood of subtle (and not so subtle) filth, relative morality, or no morality at all into our living rooms. And you can bet your Nielsen ratings it will get worse. The miracle of the splitting of the atom has blessed mankind with Hiroshima, Nagasaki, and the threat of world devastation.

The list could go on, but the point is obvious: technology and education can be wonderful things, but they can also be a curse. Technology is not truth. In fact, we need the truth to help us control our technology! Truth is more than technology or information or knowledge. Truth is more than facts. Modern man is the best user of facts in history, but he lacks truth: the understanding of the meaning of things, the perception of how things really are and what to do about them.

But Jesus says we can know the truth, and His truth can set us free. He has given us His truth in His Word. The next important step is ours. If we say, "Yes, Lord, I believe you have the truth," but we fail to learn that truth, we remain bound by our own ignorance and chained by our own frustration. How much of God's truth is really yours? Do you know where to go in the Scriptures to find the truth about God or about man or about life or about death?[2] Could you quickly locate passages that tell you His truth about relationships between men and women, husbands and wives, parents and children, or friends and enemies?[3] The Bible even gives us the truth about what to eat and drink, how to live and how to think. Do you know where it talks about these principles?[4]

In the Scriptures we can find what is right and what is wrong. We can know what really matters, what is truly meaningful and purposeful. We can learn where and how to commit our lives and know that we can count on the results. In Christ we can know the truth, continue in the truth, and be free indeed!

To Sum It Up

Jesus promises that we shall know the truth, and the truth shall set us free. We gain access to His truth by believing in Him and then holding to His teaching. The challenge for every disciple is this: "How much of the Scripture—the truth—is really mine? Am I holding to Christ's Word, or am I drifting in the twilight zone, toward the marshy ground of half-faith?"

To say that you believe the Bible is not enough. The devils believe and tremble. Some of us say that we believe and don't even twitch a little. But we ought to.

Christians don't claim to "have everything figured out." They don't need to figure it all out because God is in control. He has already given Christians the truth they need in His Word and in His Son, Jesus Christ. But in order to own the truths of the Bible and apply them, Christians must continue to hold on to the Word and to study it. Resources like the *MacArthur Study Bible* and various Bible dictionaries can assist in this process. But in the end, Christians must turn back to the Bible again and again to ground themselves in Christ's teaching, in the truth that can set them free.

Chapter Eleven

HOW DOES GOD'S WORD REVEAL THE LORD'S WILL?

Often when I get into a spiritual discussion with anyone, sooner or later we seem to get around to what God wants in a given situation. How to know God's will; how to find God's will (and sometimes how to avoid God's will) are major concerns for most Christian believers.

Along with these concerns, I often detect quite a bit of confusion. People say, "I do this because it's God's will"; and other people say, "I don't do that very same thing, because it's God's will." I heard of one fellow who advised putting all the arguments for doing something in one column and all the arguments against it in the other column. Whichever column came out the longest was the way to go! You don't have to read the daily papers very long until you see that God's will—or what people think is God's will—gets blamed for much bizarre and even tragic behavior.

Then a lot of people I talk with seem to think that God's will has been misplaced. They keep telling me, "I'm searching for God's will." Whenever I hear that I ask, "Is it lost?" The concept of searching for God's will makes it seem as though God might be the big Easter bunny in the sky. He hops around the universe stashing His will under some supernatural bush, while we run through life trying to find it. Every now and then He calls down, "You're getting warmer!"

Still other people see God as sort of a cosmic killjoy, always making people do something miserable or boring. Then there is also the casual catch-the-brass-ring-on-the merry-go-round-of-life approach, which says, "If you find the will of God, that's great. But if you don't, there's nothing to worry about. You're still going to heaven."

With all these concepts and misconceptions, what *is* God's will? Can we actually know? Can we pin it down? Does God really have a will for your life and mine? I believe He does and that He hasn't hidden it anywhere. If God has a will, He will reveal it.

There are any number of formulas and systems dealing with how God reveals His will. Some of them are excellent, such as *Getting to Know the Will of God*, by Alan Redpath. He compares finding God's will to sailing a ship according to three navigation lights: the Bible; the inward witness of the Holy Spirit; and outward circumstances. When all three lights are in line with one another, it is all right to proceed.[1]

In his helpful book *Living God's Will,* Dwight L. Carlson lists at least ten specific steps for knowing the will of God: being obedient, being open, using God's Word, prayer, the Holy Spirit, counsel from others, providential circumstances, evaluation, deciding, and having peace.[2]

Interestingly enough; all three of the systems I've mentioned talk about using Scripture. Some years ago I decided to do my own study to determine what the will of God is for believers, *according to His own Word.* The formulas were useful, but I kept wondering, What does the Bible actually say about "God's will"?

So I went to the Scriptures and studied every passage I could find on God's will. I discovered five basic principles every Christian can use to know God's will for his or her life.

Principle One: Be Saved

Primary among those things God wills, according to His Word, is this promise from 2 Peter: "The Lord . . . is longsuffering . . . not willing that any should perish, but that all should come to repentance" (2 Pet. 3:9). You find that same thought in 1 Timothy where Paul says that God "desires all men to be saved and to come to the knowledge of the truth" (1 Tim. 2:4).

Actually, salvation is where the will of God begins. Jesus makes this very clear in a brief passage in Mark. His mother and brothers arrive where He is teaching and begin asking for Him. The crowd tells Him: "Your mother and Your brothers are outside seeking You" (Mark 3:32). Jesus replies, "Who is my mother, or My brothers?" (Mark 3:33). Then, looking at those seated around Him listening to His Word, He answers His own question: "Here are My mother and My brothers! For whoever does the will of God is My brother and My sister and mother" (Mark 3:34).

What Jesus was saying was this: "The will of God is that you be related to me through faith, not through human family ties."

How willing was God that we be saved? "But God, who is rich in mercy, because of His great love with which He loved us, even when we were dead in trespasses, made us alive together with Christ (by grace you have been saved)" (Eph. 2:4). God was so willing for all to be saved that He sent His own Son to die, to make His will possible.

Unfortunately, telling people that it's God's will that they be saved isn't always popular. I can recall when I took part in an evangelism "blitz" on the campus of UCLA. We made quite a stir by witnessing to everyone and anyone we could find. The next day the *Daily Bruin*, the campus newspaper, carried a major story and a cartoon showing the Bruin mascot lying on the ground with a Christian's heel in his neck, as if the Christian had slain the poor little bear. The Christian was labeled as a Christian in a fashion that unmistakably reminded us of KKK—Klu Klux Klan.

Included in the article was a quote by the dean who said that there would be disciplinary action if the blitz was not stopped immediately. He also quoted from the university charter, which said the campus "was not to be used for religious conversion." We stopped, of course, but we found it all a bit ironic. Students can attend UCLA and come out atheists, agnostics, or psychological basket cases because they feel totally alienated from God and their fellowman, but "getting saved" is against the rules. You have to go across the street to do that.

Why is getting saved so unpopular on a secular campus? Because getting saved deals with sin, and secular man does not want to respond to any message that talks about his sin. But this is where it all starts. Until you know Jesus Christ personally, you have never taken the first step into the will of God.

Principle Two: Be Spirit-Filled

According to God's Word, a second step toward God's will is to be Spirit-filled. In the fifth chapter of his letter designed to help the Ephesian Christians resist slipping back into legalism, Paul says: "See then that you walk circumspectly, not as fools but as wise, redeeming the time, because the days are evil. Therefore do not be unwise, but understand what the will of the Lord is. And do not be drunk with wine, in which is dissipation; but be filled with the Spirit" (Eph. 5:15–18).

I used to wonder why Paul would contrast being filled with the Spirit with getting drunk. Somehow, it didn't seem appropriate. But then I finally got the point. When you get drunk you submit yourself to the control of alcohol, which permeates your system. And when the alcohol takes over, you become the kind of person alcohol influences you to be. That's what "under the influence" means. And it is also clear that the pagans of Paul's day believed drunkenness enhanced their communion with their gods. Paul shows that it is not wine that does that but the Holy Spirit. He opens us up to God.

I had a friend who was an alcoholic. From the time he was seventeen until he was twenty-two I doubt he was sober more than two weeks at a time. While sober he was quiet, meek, and mild. When intoxicated he turned into someone else. One night he called me, raving drunk, so I went over to try to help him. When I walked in he picked up a bottle of Jack Daniels and sailed it across the room right at me. I ducked, and it splattered all over the wall. I decided to leave and come back later when he was a little less under the influence of "old Jack" and his friends.

Paul uses the graphic negative example of being drunk to illustrate what it means to be filled with the Spirit. When you yield control of yourself to alcohol, it takes over. And when you are Spirit-filled, obviously the Spirit takes over. In both cases "self-control" is gone and replaced by something or someone else. In both cases there is total yieldedness to a power within. And the amazing thing about being under control of the Spirit is that you don't even have to ask questions, you just operate within the will of God.

One way to get a practical handle on the Spirit-filled life is to see it as living every single moment in the conscious presence of Jesus Christ. The Spirit-filled life is no great mystery; it is simply Christ-consciousness.

One note of caution, however: To be Christ conscious does not mean walking around muttering, "I know you're there . . . I know you're there . . . I know you're there." That's the legalistic, fetish approach that was used by the Pharisees. They were sometimes called "the bruised and bleeding Pharisees," a name they picked up because they thought it was a sin to look upon a woman. Every time a woman came along, they closed their eyes, muttered something about "I can't look . . . I can't look" and walked smack into a wall or a tree!

No, being Spirit-filled is a matter of living every day, with your eyes wide open, saturated with the presence of Christ. And how do you get saturated? It's by studying His Word. The more I focus on Christ in the Word of God, the more the thoughts of God saturate my mind; the more God's thoughts saturate my mind, the more yielded I am to Him. It is the same as letting "the Word of Christ dwell in you richly" (Col. 3:16).

Unfortunately, when it comes to God's will a lot of Christians skip this crucial step of being Spirit-filled. Instead they jump right over to wondering if they should marry Suzy or George, go to this school, take that job, buy that kind of car, and so on. They pray and pray for God's will, and they still haven't yielded control to the Holy Spirit. No, God's will is not lost or hidden. It's there in plain sight in His Word—be saved, then Spirit-filled!

Principle Three: Be Sanctified

A third clear teaching in God's Word about His will concerns our sanctification, or in simpler and more useful terms, our purity and holiness. While writing to the Christians at Thessalonica, Paul said: "For this is the will of God, your sanctification: that you should abstain from sexual immorality; that each of you should know how to possess his own vessel in sanctification and honor, not in passion of lust, like the Gentiles who do not know God" (1 Thess. 4:3–5).

Purity and holiness are often uncomfortable terms for Christians. They sound so self-righteous and sanctimonious. Actually, purity and holiness are two crucial parts of practical Christian living.

In 1 Thessalonians 4:3, 4, you can find several principles for purity. The first one is plain enough: "Avoid sexual immorality." Stay away from sexual sins. Did Paul mean sex was evil? Of course not. Sex is a beautiful, glorious human relationship—within marriage. But sexual immorality ("fornication" in some versions) refers to sexual sin outside the marriage bond, everything from premarital sex to perversions like bisexuality and homosexuality.

There is a tendency, of course, on the part of older adults to relegate most sexual sins to the young. Adults in their thirties and older cluck concernedly over the escapades of the teenagers and couples in their twenties, who are living together without benefit of marriage.

But sexual temptations and living-together arrangements are not the exclusive possession of youth. In fact, there may be *more* problems among those in their thirties, forties, and fifties. The struggles of *Men in Mid-Life Crisis* have been well documented by Jim Conway.[3] And, of course, the women are having their problems, too. As one wife put it: "All of a sudden . . . I've noticed the streets are full of men. . . . For years I must've been going by them with my eyes closed, but now I see them all right. I hardly see anything else."[4]

No matter what your age, the sex drive is a powerful force. If the Holy Spirit is not in control, it is too easy to go over the line. Where is the line? When you have to start asking that, you've probably gone over it already.

Another principle for purity in 1 Thessalonians 4:4 simply adds that "each of you" should control his (or her) own body. There are no exceptions, no special privileges. There are people, who don't engage directly in immorality, but they entertain themselves by watching others who do. I recall hearing a group of students at a Christian college who decided to use their Christian liberty to watch a pornographic film. Of course, they made a lot of noises about how they would never do what they were watching. But if you go out and watch it, you may as well have done it as far as its effect on your purity is concerned.

Keep in mind, also, that while you may be able to say you have never gone to such a film, you may be watching the same thing in principle right in your living room. Television becomes more loaded with violence, soft pornography, and other trash with each new season. What are you watching?

Today, evil, lust, and immorality come in all kinds of wrappings. God's will, according to 1 Thessalonians 4:3, 4 is that no Christian should be entertained, interested, or enticed by it. Christian purity and holiness is not sanctimonious, self-righteous drivel. It concerns how we live our daily lives; and it is a crucial part of doing God's will. If we are running around trying to find God's specific answers for certain questions but are living impure lives, why should God give us those answers when we still haven't obeyed His will that He has already revealed?

God's will is that we be saved, Spirit-filled, and sanctified—set apart as pure and holy people fit for His use.

Principle Four: Be Submissive

God's will also covers being submissive. No, this doesn't mean only the wives; I'm talking about Peter's teaching, which advises everyone to "submit yourselves to every ordinance of man for the Lord's sake, whether to the king as supreme, or to governors, as to those who are sent by him for the punishment of evildoers and *for the* praise of those who do good. For this is the will of God, that by doing good you may put to silence the ignorance of foolish men" (1 Pet. 2:13–15).

In so many words Peter is telling us, "Obey the law." But are we sure we are hearing Peter correctly? Submit ourselves to every authority, every law of man? What if we don't agree? And what about that scene in Acts where Peter and the other apostles were hauled into court and ordered to quit preaching and teaching about Christ? Didn't Peter say, "We ought to obey God rather than men" (Acts 5:29)?

There might be those times when we have to choose between obeying God and the government, but Peter isn't talking about that here in his letter. He is talking about being a good citizen and thus a good witness for Christ. That's why he goes on to say, live "as free, yet not using liberty as a cloak for vice, but as bondservants of God. Honor all people. Love the brotherhood. Fear God. Honor the king" (1 Pet. 2:16, 17).

I talked with one fellow while visiting a prison. He came up after I preached and told me what a fine message it was, that he had been a Christian for years. So I asked him why he was doing time, and he explained that he had failed to pay thirty traffic fines, plus a few other fines, all the while professing Christianity. As kindly as possible, I told him that until he could get his life shaped up, it would probably be better if people didn't know he was a Christian. It's true that God's grace can easily supersede thirty traffic tickets, but this man's inconsistency and apparent insincerity were being a poor testimony, to say the least.

Not only are we to pay our taxes, obey the traffic laws, and support the other laws of the land, but Peter also talks about being submissive on the job: "Servants, be submissive to your masters with all fear, not only to the good and gentle, but also to the harsh" (1 Pet. 2:18). Granted, most people don't have to live in slavery today, but then again some of us work for employers whom we refer to as slave drivers. No matter, says Peter, submit anyway. Why? So we can be a good advertisement for Jesus Christ.

If we are going to be Christians and do God's will, submission is part of the package. We live in an ungodly system, and it is God's will we try to live as exemplary people. That not only includes obeying laws and obeying employers, it also includes, Peter says, showing respect to everyone. I heard a story that nicely illustrates the need to be less belligerent, less uptight, and just plain more agreeable people. It seems this Christian fellow was driving along the street when someone pulled up behind him and started pounding on his horn.

Beep, beep, beep!

Apparently our Christian friend wasn't driving all that fast, and he probably thought he had "some impatient jerk" behind him who wanted to get by. Beep, be-e-ep, beep!

So he started fuming and finally couldn't stand it any longer. They came to a red light and he stopped, jumped out, ran back to the "mad honker" on his tail, and said, "If you don't quit blowing that horn, I'll . . ." About then the guy in the other car said, "Oh, I'm sorry. I saw your bumper sticker, 'Honk if you love Jesus.' So of course, I honked!" It's as true with this submissive principle as it was with the others. If we are looking for God's specific guidance and are not being the kind of citizens we ought to be, the kind of employees we ought to be, or the kind of people we ought to be in relating to others, we are missing it. We are to obey God's clearly stated will: be saved, Spirit-filled, sanctified, and submissive. The rest takes care of itself.

Principle Five: Suffer for Christ's Sake

The fifth and last principle the Bible teaches about God's will is that we are to willingly suffer. Almost all of us think we qualify here. All of us think we have to suffer through the indignities someone puts us through, whether the person is our mother-in-law or our kids.

Peter, however, wasn't writing about our everyday discomforts and frustrations in the following passage. Peter wrote his two letters to Christians who were suffering for their faith. That's why he says:

> Beloved, do not think it strange concerning the fiery trial which is to try you, as though some strange thing happened to you; but rejoice

> to the extent that you partake of Christ's sufferings, that when His glory is revealed, you may also be glad with exceeding joy. If you are reproached for the name of Christ, blessed are you, for the Spirit of glory and of God rests upon you. On their part He is blasphemed, but on your part He is glorified. But let none of you suffer as a murderer, a thief, an evildoer, or as a busybody in other people's matters. Yet if anyone suffers as a Christian, let him not be ashamed, but let him glorify God in this matter. . . Therefore let those who suffer according to the will of God commit their souls to Him in doing good, as to a faithful Creator. (1 Pet. 4:12–16, 19)

If you're not getting along with your spouse, or your relatives, or your pastor, it's more than likely partly your fault. What Peter is talking about is *suffering for good*—for living a godly life in an ungodly society. Do that, and you are bound to get some hack. When you go out and confront the world boldly for Jesus Christ and suffer for it, that is God's will.

Granted, few of us, in the Western world at least, know much about suffering for Jesus, including myself. I did get one taste of it, however, when I preached on a secular junior college campus on the topic, "Christianity and Culture." I talked on culture for a while and then switched to talking about why Jesus is the Messiah. It was a predominantly Jewish student body, so that seemed appropriate to a discussion of culture. It turned into an exciting meeting, with all kinds of antagonistic people there. But I stuck my neck out, trusted God, and told it like I believe it is.

In the next few days, I got letters with threats to bomb my church. One phone caller told us he would blow up the church during a Sunday service. I even got obscene phone calls at home in the middle of the night.

Through the experience, I got a small taste of suffering. But the best part was that some people got saved. I remember in particular a young fellow named Dan, who came to see me not long after hearing my message on "Christianity and Culture"; I led him to Christ. Eventually he became a key member of our fellowship.

Although we shouldn't seek out pain and suffering, we must be willing to take a stand, even if it means persecution and suffering. The Spirit and glory of God will rest on us in the midst of our suffering.

To Sum It Up

There is a lot of concern and confusion about God's will, but it doesn't remain a mystery. God's will is not lost[5] neither is it the brass ring that some people catch and others miss, but in the end it really doesn't matter.

There are many good formulas and systems for learning God's will. But the best system is simply reading the Bible and finding out what it teaches about God's will:

> He wants us to be saved (see 2 Pet. 3:9).
> He wants us to be Spirit-filled (see Eph. 5:15–18).
> He wants us to be sanctified (see 1 Thess. 4:3, 4).
> He wants us to be submissive (see 1 Pet. 2:13–15).
> He wants us to be willing to suffer for His sake (see 1 Pet. 4:12–19).

About now you might be saying, "All these biblical principles are fine; but they're general. What about taking a new job, picking a mate, buying a new car or house, and the million other decisions that involve my Christian walk and testimony?"

Well, I've got one other principle for doing God's will, and it may sound too good to be true. If you are saved, Spirit-filled, sanctified, submissive, and willing to suffer, do whatever you want. Whatever you want? That's right. If you are obeying God's Word in the five areas discussed in this chapter, God is *already* controlling your wants and desires. He is at work "in you both to will and to do for His good pleasure" (Phil. 2:13). If you "delight . . . in the LORD," He will give you "the desires of your heart" (Ps. 37:4) because they will be His desires for you.

Chapter Twelve

How Does God's Word Help Us Grow Spiritually?

Have you ever met someone who hasn't matured? It's a sad sight, for example, to meet someone thirty years old with the mind of a baby still in diapers. Because of brain damage or some other disorder, these people just don't develop. Their bodies grow to some extent, but they remain virtual infants as far as the rest of their growth and maturity is concerned.

Something almost as disheartening is to see Christians who don't develop. Spiritually they remain retarded, stunted, never becoming what God has in mind for them to be. If you challenge these believers, they will deny that their goal is little or no growth. (In fact, they may indignantly argue that they *are* growing—at their own pace!) Everybody wants to grow; it's just that some people want to grow with no effort. That's where the problem lies.

While I was in college, I wasted my time and didn't grow spiritually very much, if at all. But when I got to seminary I got a taste of God's Word in a new and different way. During those seminary days, I learned to study the Bible systematically. That's when I began to grow. Ever since that time I have found that my spiritual growth is directly proportionate to the amount of time and effort I put into the study of Scripture. Many Christians to whom I've ministered or with whom I have worked would agree.

When believers aren't growing, it can usually be traced to a failure to be in God's Word. They go to church and sit. They complain of not getting much out of church or the Christian life. They are weak and run down when it comes to facing temptations, trials, problems, and challenges. They lack the energy to do much of anything for the Lord.

Their souls are starved for wholesome spiritual food. The Bible refers to itself as milk, bread, and meat, but spiritually a lot of Christians are subsisting on cola, french fries, and candy. They aren't growing because they refuse to feed themselves. Ironically, the solution to their problems is in the very thing they refuse to feed upon—God's Word.

How to Eat Right and Grow Spiritually

There are several excellent biblical passages that talk about spiritual growth, but perhaps the best, and certainly the most basic, is in 1 Peter. Peter wrote two New Testament letters to Christians under intense persecution. Because they had been preaching that the world would be destroyed by fire, the Roman authorities were suspicious of their motives and saw them as a threat to the security of the Empire. But the thrust of Peter's message to them is clear. Don't worry. Put your hope in Christ and learn to live in the light of that, not under your present circumstances.

The Christian believers who read Peter's letters probably weren't too concerned about growing very much in their present situation. They were concentrating on survival. Yet, early in his first letter, Peter told them that part of the reason they could have hope was because of the living Word of Christ:

> Since you have purified your souls in obeying the truth through the Spirit in sincere love of the brethren, love one another fervently with a pure heart, having been born again, not of corruptible seed but incorruptible, through the word of God which lives and abides forever, because "All flesh is as grass; and all the glory of man as the flower of the grass. The grass withers; and its flower falls away; but the word of the LORD endures forever." Now this is the word which by the gospel was preached to you. Therefore, laying aside all malice, all deceit, hypocrisy, envy, and all evil speaking, as newborn babes, desire the pure

> milk of the word, that you may grow thereby, if indeed you have tasted that the Lord is gracious. (1 Pet. 1:23–2:3)

One of the many statements that the Bible makes concerning itself is that it is a living Word. In Philippians 2:16 Paul calls it the "word of life." Hebrews 4:12 says, "The word of God is living and powerful." Here in 1 Peter 1:23, it is "the word of God which lives and abides forever." There are no more significant, or more important statements, that refer to the Bible than these. It is through this living Word that we are born again and made alive spiritually. And it is through the living Word that we grow up into Christ.

The Word of God Is Alive and Produces Life

The Word of God is the only thing we know of, apart from the Trinity itself, that is alive in an eternal sense. In the world around us the things we call "living" are really dying. What we call "the land of the living" is probably better called "the land of the dying" because wherever you look, death is doing its work of decay and destruction. In the final analysis, death is the monarch of this world. Against this background of decay and death the Word of God stands forth as really being alive. The corruption of this world cannot touch God's Word; it cannot remove its validity; it cannot deteriorate its reality; it cannot decay its truth.

God's Word is alive in a truer sense than you and I are alive. As Peter quotes Isaiah 40:6–8: "All flesh is as grass; and all the glory of man as the flower of the grass. The grass withers; and its flower falls away; but the word of the LORD endures forever" (1 Pet. 1:24, 25).

One of the many indications of the life in God's Word is its perennial freshness. In every generation, to every person who picks it up, it is alive, living, and fresh. I have reread some parts of the Bible many, many times. I would hope that I had them memorized and would never need to look at them again, but in many cases I am just beginning to understand what they say. I once read the Book of Colossians every day for ninety days and, after all of that, Colossians still holds mysteries for me that I haven't tapped. Every time I read the book of Colossians I gain new excitement and fresh insights.

Something else that says God's Word is alive is that it is never obsolete. In the back of libraries, you can find all of the old, obsolete textbooks. In recent years, scientific discoveries make dozens and even hundreds of books obsolete each day. But the timeless truths of the Bible never become obsolete. They are as up to date as the next generation of men and women who need its message so desperately.

And one of the most convincing reasons to call the Word of God alive is its power. The Bible is a discerner of hearts. Scripture has a living insight into me that makes me shake. Through the Bible the Holy Spirit is able to split me wide open and reveal to me my faults, my needs, my weakness—my sins. No wonder Hebrews 4:12 tells us: "The word of God is . . . sharper than any two-edged sword, piercing even to dividing soul and spirit . . . and is a discerner of the thoughts and intents of the heart."

Most important, the Word of God is alive because it produces growth. As 1 Peter 1:23 points out, "having been born again, not of corruptible seed but incorruptible, through the word of God which lives and abides forever." The great mystery of any living being is its power to reproduce. And reproduce, says Peter, is exactly what the Word of God does. The only way to be a "son of God" is to be born by the Word of God. When the Word of God is truly heard, and sincerely received into a heart that has been prepared by God, that Word, quickened by the Holy Spirit, becomes a spiritual seed that is imperishable or incorruptible. That seed is the germ of a new creation, and it springs into life by making the hearer who believes a son of God.

Jesus illustrates the same concept in His parable of the sower in Luke 8. The farmer goes out to sow, and some seed lands on the path, some on rocky soil, some where weeds spring up, and some on good ground that produces much more. As He explains the parable to His disciples, Jesus says: "The seed is the word of God. Those by the wayside are the ones who hear; then the devil comes and takes away the word out of their hearts, lest they should believe and be saved" (Luke 8:11, 12).

The one ingredient a person must have to believe and be saved is God's Word. Naturally, it is the one ingredient that Satan wants to take away. If Satan fails to take it away, life results. Note Jesus' words in Luke 8:15: "But the ones that fell on the good ground are those who, having heard the word with a noble and good heart, keep it and bear fruit with patience." For one more scriptural confirmation of the power of the Word to bring life, see John 6:63: "It is the Spirit who gives life; the flesh profits nothing. The words that I speak to you are spirit, and they are life." The Word of God, in the hand of the Holy Spirit, is the critical life-giving agent. The Spirit of God, using the Word of God, produces life.

How to Get Off Spiritual Junk Food

One reason so many Christians suffer from spiritual malnutrition is that they live on a diet of junk food, as far as building spiritual character is concerned. Peter is well aware of this and that's why he says: "Therefore, laying aside all malice, all deceit, hypocrisy, envy, and all evil speaking" (1 Pet. 2:1). The Greek word used for "laying aside" actually means to "strip off your clothes." The same idea is expressed in Hebrews 12:1 where we are told to "lay aside every weight, and the sin which so easily ensnares us." Peter talks about five specifics that we should strip out of our lives: malice, deceit, hypocrisy, envy, and slander.

Malice was the general word for wickedness. In Peter's day it meant "heathen evil"—the characteristic evil of the world surrounding the young Christian church. Peter doesn't advise laying aside some of it; he demands *all* of it to go. Today's Christians are no different than those in the first century. Many of us like to play at Christianity and keep worldly practices and values in our lives. But there is no place in the Christian's life for the garbage of the world.

A young man once approached a great Bible teacher and said to him, "Sir, I'd give the world to know the Bible as you do."

The teacher looked him in the eye and said: "And that's exactly what it will cost you!" If we want to grow, if we want to develop to our full potential, then each of us has to look inside to recognize those worldly remnants and scraps that we are hanging on to, which are hampering growth and maturity.

All deceit also has to go, says Peter. At the root of deceit is impure motives; and this leads to conscious deception of others. But deceit always costs you in the long run, while honesty always pays.

This is a hard lesson to teach children. I tell my own children, "It's really a lot more expensive to lie, because every time I catch you in a lie you are going to be punished much more severely than if you told me the truth." I've had to prove this on occasion, and it's always a hard lesson for everyone—for me to teach and for them to learn—but it's worth it.

Hypocrisy is another attitude Christians should purge from their lives, just as people would abstain from junk food. Hypocrisy is a natural outgrowth of deceit. Non-Christians always like to point out that the church is full of hypocrites, and unfortunately they are right.

Christians sometimes reply to this charge by saying that the church—where people can hear the gospel and learn about the Bible—is the best place for hypocrites. But as Peter plainly shows us, we can't be content with merely saying, "It's good to be in church where we're learning to deal with our hypocrisy, deceit, malice, and other problems."

Never be content with keeping this garbage in your life. Strip it off! There is no place in the life of a sincere Christian for hypocrisy. If a Christian glibly excuses his hypocrisy, he is taking advantage of God's grace and is a greater hypocrite.

Envy is a fourth attitude that must be purged from a Christian's life. Reduced to its basic components, envy is simply self-centeredness. Envy is always the last attitude to die, because it only dies when the self dies. As most Christians know, the self is hard to kill.

How many churches have been wrecked, how many missionary organizations have been riddled with dissension, how many families have been destroyed, all by envy? In his letter, James joins Peter in warning Christians about the demonic influence of envy: "But if you have bitter envy and self-seeking in your hearts, do not boast and lie against the truth. This wisdom does not descend from above, but is earthly, sensual, demonic. For where envy and self-seeking exist, confusion and every evil thing are there" (James 3:14–16).

Slander of every kind (evil speaking) is a fifth attitude that has to go. In a word, Peter is telling us, "Quit your gossiping." Gossip just might be the most attractive sin for Christians. We all clatter concernedly over gossip; and we nod vigorously when the preacher condemns it from the pulpit. Yet on the way home, or even while walking to the car, after church has let out, we start gossiping. We are very clever, of course, to mask our gossip behind words such as: "I'm so concerned about Mary"; or "Can you fill me in a little, so I can pray about it?" Far too much gossip goes on under the guise of prayer.

It is worthwhile to note how all of these five items of "spiritual junk food" are all on one large menu. Each attitude seems to feed the other, just as they nourish the Christian who keeps them in his diet. The fruit of malice is very often deceit or guile; and deceit and guile lead to hypocrisy, which, in turn, produces the envy. Then the fruit of envy often leads to evil speaking—slanderous gossip. The trouble is, of course, like all junk food this garbage tastes good. We've acquired a real taste for these evil habits; and it's hard to break them. What we need is to start feeding on something else to change our taste buds; and that's what Peter talks about next.

Feed on God's Word and Grow

The obvious replacement for junk food in anyone's diet is wholesome and nourishing food. Peter knows that the cure for spiritual malnutrition is regular diet of God's Word. That's why he says: "as newborn babes, desire the pure milk of the word, that you may grow thereby, if indeed you have tasted that the Lord is gracious" (1 Pet. 2:2, 3). Peter was telling his readers they had tasted God's grace by taking that first step into salvation. The imperishable seed has sprouted, and now they need to feed the new life they have within. They should desire the Word as a baby desires milk. Milk is crucial to the growth of any baby; and God's Word is crucial to the growth of a Christian.

Paul had the same idea when he wrote to the Christians at Thessalonica and said: "But we were gentle among you, just as a nursing mother cherishes her own children" (1 Thess. 2:7). Paul communicated the same notion when he wrote Timothy to encourage him to stand fast in the face of apostasy: "If you instruct the brethren in these things, you will be a good minister of Jesus Christ, nourished in the words of faith and of the good doctrine which you have carefully followed" (1 Tim. 4:6).

Although we are to desire the Word as a baby desires milk, the Word is also meat. Just as the human body needs other foods beyond just milk to get proper nutrition, so our souls need more than spiritual milk. While some Christians are doing well with laying off spiritual junk food, they are perhaps too content with a weekly bottle of milk, fed to them by their preacher. They are failing to get into the Word of God for themselves, where they can chew on more solid food.

True spiritual nourishment for the believer is God's Word. But as Paul told the Corinthians there is more to God's Word than just milk (see 1 Cor. 3:1, 2). Milk helps us get a good start with our growth, but we also need to find solid food—the rich spiritual truths that God wants us to have so we can truly change and become what He wants us to be.

Eat All of God's Word and Watch Yourself Change

Not only do most Christians want to grow, but they also want to be different—what the Bible calls renewed or transformed into stronger, more powerful, more effective servants of Christ. That is exactly what Paul is talking about in Romans 12:2 when he says, "Do not be conformed to this world, but be transformed by the renewing of your mind." As every Christian well knows, the old mind—with its habits of self-preoccupation, its craving for sensation and vain imaginations, and its appetite for what is vile and gross—is still there.

The flesh is the culprit that keeps us going back to junk food. The flesh is the subtle enemy that keeps us feeding only on milk when we should be eating meat. The flesh is what keeps us from being transformed and interfering with our commitment to Christ and His Word. We keep going around and around and never seem to find the secret. That is because the key to the mystery lies right under our noses.

Paul gives us a clear explanation in 2 Corinthians 3:14–18. As he describes the glories of the new covenant that Christians have with God, he goes back to the time of Moses and the Israelites. At one point, after being in God's presence, Moses' face shone with such brilliant glory that he had to put a veil over it in order not to blind his people. But as glorious as Moses' ministry of the law to the Israelites was, Paul says that it does not compare with the surpassing glory of the gospel of Christ and the new covenant that He installed with His death and resurrection (see 2 Cor. 3:7–11). And Paul goes on to say that since we have such a wonderful hope in Christ we can be very bold. "Therefore, since we have such hope, we use great boldness of speech—unlike Moses, who put a veil over his face so that the children of Israel could not look steadily at the end of what was passing away. But their minds were blinded. For until this day the same veil remains unlifted in the reading of the Old Testament, because the veil is taken away in Christ" (2 Cor. 3:12–14). What Paul is simply saying here is that the Jews of his day who didn't know Christ couldn't understand the gospel because their minds were veiled. They could not see the Lord because the veil of the old covenant—the law—stood in the way.

Paul goes on to say that the veil "remains unlifted in the reading of the Old Testament, because the veil is taken away in Christ. But even to this day, when Moses is read, a veil lies on their heart. Nevertheless when one turns to the Lord, the veil is taken away. Now the Lord is the Spirit; and where the Spirit of the Lord is, there is liberty" (2 Cor. 3:14–17).

Then Paul comes to the thought that I am most concerned with: "But we all, with unveiled face, beholding as in a mirror the glory of the Lord, are being transformed into the same image from glory to glory, just as by the Spirit of the Lord" (2 Cor. 3:18). Thus Paul tells us that we can be changed into the image and glory of the Lord. It is very simple, he says. We don't change ourselves. We just stand staring into the face of Jesus Christ, and the Spirit of God does the transforming for us!

You may be saying there's just one hitch: "If I'm supposed to look on the glory of the Lord, where do I find it to look upon?" And, of course, the answer to that is *in God's Word.*

If you keep learning and beholding the glory of God in His Word, the Spirit of God will transform you into the image of Jesus Christ. It is just that simple (and just that difficult). Many Christians, however, are seeking shortcuts to growth. In recent days, they have even been trying to make quantum leaps to "super spirituality." But the shortcut simply doesn't exist.

The greatest event that ever happened in my life, next to my salvation, was the day I learned to study God's Word. I find that the longer, the more intensely, and the more devotedly I look into the glory of Jesus Christ through the pages of Scripture, the more the Spirit of God changes my life into the image of Christ. There are no shortcuts. If I am to grow, to mature, and to finally be transformed, I must feed on the Word of God.

To Sum It Up

Lack of growth is sad to see in anyone or anything. It is especially tragic in Christians, but unfortunately too many believers don't seem to be growing very much in their faith. The major cause of their lack of growth is failure to read and study God's Word.

In 1 Peter 1:23–2:3, the great apostle compares God's Word to two things that are vital for life and growth: an imperishable seed and the milk of the Word. As Christ taught in His parable of the sower, God's Word is like a seed that brings about new birth. Just as a seed contains the power and energy of life, so does God's Word.

Before a Christian can get the most from feeding on God's Word, he or she needs to get rid of the "junk food diet" that is so tasty to the flesh that all believers still have within them. Peter describes this junk food diet as the evils of worldly malice, the guile of deceitfulness, and the phoniness of hypocrisy, the self-centeredness of envy, and the slander of gossip. If we want to change our diet, we should start with the sincere milk of the Word of God. We need to spend time reading the Bible. We need to study it with the assistance of Bible helps, such as the *MacArthur Study Bible,* Bible dictionaries, and various commentaries. Fully immersing ourselves in God's Word will guarantee our spiritual growth.

Our goal is to become fully mature and transformed through feeding on the solid food found in Scripture. An accurate description and watchword for any Christian can be found in Jeremiah 15:16: "Your words were found, and I ate them; and Your word was to me the joy and rejoicing of my heart; for I am called by Your name, O LORD God of hosts."

Chapter Thirteen
How Does God's Word Make Us Productive?

How much fruit are you bearing in your Christian life? Occasionally when I ask believers a question like that, I get blank or guilty looks. Some are not sure what I mean. Fruit? They don't own an orchard; they're lucky if they can keep the dust off the rose bushes. Others think I want them to whip out a list of souls won to Christ this month; and because their list is quite short—or nonexistent—they feel guilty.

What, then, is Christian fruit? Does it have something to do with the fruit of the Spirit? Just how does a Christian bear fruit in daily living? And, what part does God's Word play in all this?

He Is the Vine; We Are the Branches

The classical biblical passage on Christian fruit-bearing is John 15:1–8. Jesus and His disciples are in the Upper Room on the night before His death. As they are about to leave, the Lord stops and says:

> I am the true vine, and My Father is the vinedresser. Every branch in Me that does not bear fruit He takes away; and every branch that bears fruit He prunes, that it may bear more fruit. You are already clean because of the word which I have spoken to you. Abide in Me, and I in you. As the branch cannot bear fruit of itself, unless it abides in the vine, neither can you, unless you abide in Me. I am the vine, you are the branches. He who abides in Me, and I in him, bears much fruit; for without Me you can do nothing. If anyone does not abide in Me, he is

> cast out as a branch and is withered; and they gather them and throw them into the fire, and they are burned. If you abide in Me, and My words abide in you, you will ask what you desire, and it shall be done for you. By this My Father is glorified, that you bear much fruit; so you will be My disciples. (John 15:1–8)

Here is one of the most meaningful and, at the same time, most difficult analogies in the entire Bible. Here also is one of the richest passages in the New Testament on living the Christian life.

Jesus is the vine, and His Father is the gardener—or vinedresser. The disciples are the branches. He was speaking of the eleven disciples who were still with Him as He prepared to go to the Garden of Gethsemane. They were the branches who were remaining with Him to the end. The branches who didn't bear fruit and were cut off are represented by Judas, who had already left in order to betray Jesus to the Jewish leaders later that evening. Jesus used the vine illustration for at least three good reasons:

First, His disciples would recognize the analogy immediately because Israel was often referred to as a vine in the Old Testament Scriptures. For example, Isaiah wrote: "The vineyard of the LORD of hosts is the house of Israel" (Is. 5:7). Jeremiah, speaking for God, said: "I had planted you a noble vine, a seed of highest quality" (Jer. 2:21).

Second, grapevines grew everywhere in Palestine. Some commentators, in fact, believe Jesus stopped at the doorway on His way out of the Upper Room to refer to a vine growing by the doorway.[1] When He spoke of pruning procedures, He was describing exactly what vinedressers did to produce good crops of grapes. Young vines were pruned severely for their first three years, then they were allowed to bear a crop. Mature vines were pruned every December and January. Non-fruit-bearing branches were cut back mercilessly to preserve the strength of the plant. And, as Jesus pointed out in His analogy, the wood of the pruned branches was good for nothing except making bonfires.[2]

Third, the vine and its branches perfectly illustrate the kind of relationship that must exist between Jesus and anyone who wants to be His disciple. Although Jesus was addressing His inner circle of eleven disciples, this analogy is for all Christians. Jesus is saying we have a choice: to be real branches who truly remain with Jesus and bear fruit or to be phony unproductive branches who appear to be connected to the vine but are not. Like Judas, these phony branches will fade away and produce no fruit at all. Their ultimate fate is destruction.

It's important to note that Jesus says, "I am the *true* vine." In the Old Testament, Israel had been referred to as a vine planted, tended, and pruned by God. But Israel had become unproductive. In fact, the symbol of the vine used in Old Testament passages always refers to the idea of degeneration. Hosea cried that Israel was "an empty vine" (Hos. 10:1). Now, with the Old Testament order ending and the new covenant just installed at the Last Supper, Jesus states clearly that He is the true vine. It is to Him that God' s children must now be related. For anyone to know life and bear fruit, that person must be connected to Jesus Christ.

The Work of the Gardener

The task of the gardener (or vinedresser) is crucial to understanding the vine and branches analogy. The gardener is the Father who has two ministries concerning the branches on the vine—concerning those who claim allegiance to Jesus Christ.[3]

In the first century, a vinedresser would have two duties: to cut off branches that bear no fruit and to prune the fruit-bearing branches in order to help them bear even more fruit.

The word "prune" also means to purge, or to cleanse. The vinedresser would cleanse the fruit-bearing branches in various ways. Sometimes he would use his thumb and forefinger to pinch away the growing tip of a vigorous, but unwanted, shoot. Sometimes he would "top" the branch, by lopping off a foot or two to keep it from growing too large or too long and possibly snapping off in the wind. At other times, he would "thin" the vine, by removing unwanted flower clusters.

The vinedresser's one goal in all this was to make the plant more productive, to make it bear more and better fruit.

When we compare the vinedresser's work with an actual grapevine to the Father's work with us, we can see there are two kinds of Christians, just as there are two kinds of branches. First there are those who claim to follow Christ but are not true believers. Second there are those who truly believe and who bear at least some fruit in their lives. The fate of the non-fruit-bearing branches gives us an awesome warning. Those who are "Judas branches," those who do not really believe in and remain with Christ, are to be cast into eternal fire. It is not a question of these people losing their salvation. They were never saved in the first place. Sooner or later they show their real colors; and their end is destruction.

True believers, however, always bear fruit. Every Christian bears some kind of fruit. It may not be much. With some Christians you may have to look a long time to find a few lingering grapes, but they are there. If there is no fruit at all, that person is not a true Christian. The essence of the Christian life is that it must be spiritually productive in some way (see Eph. 2:10). A person may appear as if he is connected to Jesus Christ; but if he doesn't bear any fruit he is not really connected to Christ at all.

The Father's work with the fruit-bearing branches is another matter. Here He carefully prunes the Christian, trimming away sins, hindrances, and evil habits in order to help that Christian gain maximum fruit-bearing capacity.

One of the most effective ways the Father prunes the Christian is with trouble, even pain and suffering. This is not to say that every Christian who is ill, or suffering, is necessarily being pruned, but in many cases the Father allows trial and trouble to come our way in order to clean out our lives in certain areas.

Unfortunately, pruning has to be done with a knife; and therefore pruning is always painful. There are times when we wonder if God knows what He is doing because it hurts so much it seems more than we can bear. And sometimes we wonder why God seems to be doing an awful lot of pruning on our branch, while other Christians don't experience the same type of pruning. But all we can do is trust. The Father knows what He is doing. The valuable lessons He teaches us through suffering, trials, and troubles awaken us to the changes we need to make—what we need to add to our lives and what we need to remove.

The Father causes this pruning in many ways. It can be anything from sickness to hardships, such as the loss of a job. It can be the loss of a loved one or of a good friend. Pruning can come through frustration, disappointment, pressure, and stress. God ordains all kinds of troubles in order to clean off those unwanted shoots—those habits, attitudes, and practices that drain away our energy and rob us of our fruit-bearing capacity. God doesn't do this pruning with glee or vengeance. He is not the Great Slasher in the Sky, flailing away with His giant blade, snarling, "Bear more fruit, or else!" No, He is right at our side, the Gardener, who carefully prunes each of us at the right spots so we can bear more fruit.

The pruning knife may hurt now and then, but it's worth it. Have you ever thought about what the Father's pruning knife actually is? Is it suffering, troubles, or frustrations? I don't think it is any of those. John 15:3 tells me the pruning knife is the Word of God. Jesus says: "You are already clean because of the word I have spoken to you." I believe that in this verse Jesus is referring to two kinds of cleansing for His disciples. First, their initial salvation comes through hearing the Word. Second, their continual purging and pruning is done by the Word. That is why He says next: "Abide in Me, and I in you. As the branch cannot bear fruit of itself, unless it abides in the vine, neither can you, unless you abide in Me" (John 15:4).

And just how do we remain in Christ and have Him remain in us? It is *by being in the Word.* There are no substitutes, no gimmicks, no shortcuts. God's pruning knife is His Word, and as pointed out above, He seems to use it often during trouble, distress, or setbacks.

Charles Spurgeon, master preacher of the nineteenth century, said: "It is the Word that prunes the Christian. It is the truth that purges him."

Have you ever noticed how much more sensitive you are to the Word of God when trouble comes? Have you ever noticed that, when you have a particular need or problem, certain verses will leap off the page? That's the Spirit of God applying them to your heart.

What Isn't Christian Fruit

With all this pruning and purging going on, it makes sense to be sure we know what kind of fruit we are supposed to bear. One principle is basic: for the believer in Christ, bearing fruit is a requirement, not an option. The Old Testament talks about it at least seventy times. Paul talks about it in all of his letters in one way or another.

But what kind of fruit do Paul and other writers of Scripture describe? First, let's take a quick look at what Christian fruit is *not*. People shouldn't get plastic fruit confused with the real thing.[4]

Fruit is not success. Nowhere in the Bible is Christian fruit synonymous with success. We all have the tendency to think if a church is big, or if a lot of people are coming to it, that means it is bearing spiritual fruit. Not necessarily. A large, "successful" operation could be a performance of the flesh—a human effort but not real spiritual fruit at all.

On the other side of the coin, the missionary who has worked for thirty years in some backwoods, out-of-the-way place may only have three converts to his credit. It is entirely possible that his work has borne real spiritual fruit, despite the outward lack of "success."

Fruit is not sensationalism. We also tend to be impressed with the flashy, the spectacular, and the overly zealous. The emotional pitch and the ringing rhetoric all promise, "Here is real fruit!" But talk is cheap; real spiritual fruit is expensive.

Fruit is not simulation. A subtle trap ensnares many Christians when they try to imitate the actions, or style, of another believer who is apparently bearing spiritual fruit. But every Christian has to bear his or her own fruit. Each Christian is unique and so is the fruit that person bears. When Christians try to simulate, or imitate, somebody else's fruit, they violate the basic principle of abiding in Christ. Instead of living in Christ and allowing Christ to live in them and bear fruit through them, they are figuratively tying on plastic fruit to themselves. It may look good, but its taste is flat.

What Real Christian Fruit Is

Scripture describes genuine spiritual fruit in several ways, and I place them in a certain order of priority for an important reason.

First, fruit is Christlike character. Paul put it in one sentence in Galatians 5:22: "The fruit of the Spirit is love, joy, peace, patience, kindness, goodness, faithfulness, gentleness, self-control." This list describes the character traits of Jesus Christ. We are to reproduce the life of Christ in us as we abide in the vine. Jesus said: "I am the vine, you are the branches. He who abides in Me, and I in him, bears much fruit; for without Me you can do nothing" (John 15:5). To underline the absolute necessity to be in Christ—to be a "real" branch—Jesus repeats the grim warning He gave in John 15:2: "If anyone does not abide in Me, he is cast out as a branch and is withered; and they gather them and throw *them* into the fire, and they are burned" (John 15:6).

But to bear the fruit of the Spirit, or any other kind of Christian fruit, we must understand one principle. The way to fruitfulness is through Christ. One of the most frustrating tasks in the world is to try to bear the fruit of the Spirit on our own. We look at our lives and see that we are a bit short on Christian love. So, we grunt and groan and try to produce more love. Or we detect that we don't have Christian peace in our lives, so we work so hard at producing more peace that we get more uptight than ever.

Jesus doesn't tell us: "Get out there and bear more fruit!" He simply instructs us to abide, to remain with Him, and fruit will appear of its own accord.

Another description of fruit is praising the Lord in worship. Hebrews 13:15 tells us: "Therefore by Him let us continually offer the sacrifice of praise to God, that is, the fruit of our lips, giving thanks to His name." As we thank God in a spirit of worship, fruit is present. As we pray and express adoration to the Lord, that is fruit. But note that all of this is done through Jesus, not ourselves.

A third kind of fruit is good works. We often shy away from the idea of "works" because we know that we are saved by grace, not works, lest any of us might boast that we accomplished our salvation, and not God (see Eph. 2:8, 9). We forget, however, that Paul goes right on to say in Ephesians that "we are [God's] workmanship, created in Christ Jesus for good works, which God prepared beforehand that we should walk in them" (Eph. 2:10). We are not saved by our works, but we are saved to do good works in Christ's name. That is why, in his letter to the Colossian Christians, Paul tells them and, also, us:

> For this reason we also, since the day we heard it, do not cease to pray for you, and to ask that you may be filled with the knowledge of His will in all wisdom and spiritual understanding; that you may walk worthy of the Lord, fully pleasing Him, being fruitful in every good work and increasing in the knowledge of God. (Col. 1:9, 10)

Note again that Paul is praying that God will fill believers with the knowledge of His will, with spiritual wisdom and understanding. As we are filled by God, we can dispense good works that bear real fruit. And we are filled by staying close to Christ—remaining in Him.

Finally, the Christian bears fruit by winning others to Christ. A key passage that identifies those won to Christ as fruit is found in John 4. Jesus' disciples plead with Him to stop to eat, but Jesus replied that His food was doing the will of His Father and accomplishing God's work. Then Jesus said: "Do you not say, 'There are still four months and then comes the harvest'? Behold, I say to you, lift up your eyes and look at the fields, for they are already white for harvest! And he who reaps receives wages, and gathers fruit for eternal life" (John 4:35, 36).

Unfortunately, some believers think the best way to reap the harvest is to wade in and try to mow down as many converts as possible.

But the way to bear fruit as a soul winner is not by running around buttonholing people, dropping tracts on the table for the waitress instead of a tip, and so on. Instead remain in Christ. Let Him build His character in you, and the opportunities will come. Concentrate on Him; and He will place you in witnessing situations designed especially for you.

The other approach—do-it-yourself soul-winning—is a dead end. I got a taste of this while taking a summer college course in evangelism. Our assignment was to witness to seven people a week. The instructor didn't set a quota on how many we had to get converted in order to earn an A, but we were required to witness to seven people a week in order to get a grade at all. It was legalism pure and simple; but it taught me something: the folly of witnessing "because you have to" and the common sense of remaining in Christ and witnessing with what overflows into your life from knowing and loving Him. That is why the fruits of Christlike character—praising God and good works—should come first. If we aren't enjoying these fruits and seeing them fulfilled in our lives the answer is painful but obvious: we aren't abiding enough; we are not in the written or living Word enough.

Do God's Words Control Your Life?

If we are to be real, not phony branches, we must let the words of the Lord control us. And what are the words of the Lord? Do we all need to memorize the red-letter passages of red-letter Bibles? That's not a bad idea, but the words of Christ are not limited to quotes attributed to Him in red-letter editions of the Bible. As we saw in the early chapters of this book, all of Scripture has infallible, inerrant authority for our lives. What Jesus said personally isn't more important than what He said through Paul, Peter, James, Jude, and other writers of inspired Scripture. But to simply talk about "being controlled by the Word of God" remains only talk unless we can say we are actually familiar with it. There is no magic in memorizing Scripture. (In fact, it can lead you into legalism.) But there is tremendous blessing and power in knowing where various passages can be found and what kind of help and resources they can provide.

For example, the following is a brief quiz containing twelve essential Scripture passages that should be familiar to every Christian. See if you can match the right passage with the right description:

The Ten Commandments	Luke 10
The Love Chapter	Matthew 22:34–40
The Beatitudes	Matthew 5–7
The Parable of the Good Samaritan	Exodus 20
The Two Great Commandments	1 Corinthians 13
The Sermon on the Mount	Matthew 5:1–12
The Call of Abraham	Luke 6:31
The Fall of Man	Genesis 12
The Golden Rule	Luke 15
The Parable of the Prodigal Son	Genesis 3

Correct answers are listed at the end of this chapter. See how you did at matching them up. Then try covering up one column or the other and reciting the right answers from memory. Remember, memorizing verses and references can be a legalistic "head trip," if you make it that. On the other hand just what does it mean to know Christ's Word well enough to be under His control? Unless we are in the Word, reading it, memorizing it, learning what it means by reading study Bibles, such as the *MacArthur Study Bible*, and then finally, truly knowing it, all of our talk about abiding and fruit-bearing is just hot air. According to John 15:8, there is a marvelous blessing in being pruned to bear more fruit: "By this My Father is glorified, that you bear much fruit; so you will be My disciples." The believer who bears fruit through his relationship to Christ and not his own efforts and cleverness—that believer brings glory to God.

Here is the bottom line. To paraphrase the well-known answer to the first question in the Westminster Confession: He is the vine, we are the branches. By staying with Him and in Him we shall glorify God, enjoy Him forever, and show the world we are His disciples.[5]

To Sum It Up

Jesus gives us the secret of bearing fruit when He tells us that our relationship to Him must be like branches in a vine. If we are real branches, truly attached to Him in genuine faith, we will bear fruit, even if it's only a small amount. In order to help us bear more fruit, the Father uses the Word to purge and prune the unneeded habits, attitudes, and practices from our lives. He often works through trouble—anything from illness and loss to frustration and stress. His pruning knife is painful, but it's worth it.

Plastic fruit is a danger Christians must avoid. Real fruit is not necessarily success or sensationalism. Real fruit is not gained by simulating the ministry of another Christian who is bearing fruit. Every Christian is to bear his or her own fruit.

The Bible describes real fruit in several ways: (1) as Christlike character (the fruit of the Spirit); (2) as praise through worship; (3) as being fruitful in every good work. A fourth important kind of fruit is converts won to Christ, but witnessing for Him should come out of remaining in Him, not legalistic efforts.

The benefits of being pruned are many. Bearing fruit brings happiness, joy, satisfaction, and excitement. We also experience answers to prayer as our lives are regulated by God's Word. The total result is that we bring glory to God as we know and enjoy Him forever.

Answers to the quiz: the Ten Commandments—Exodus 20; the Love Chapter—1 Corinthians 13; the Beatitudes—Matthew 5:1–12; the Parable of the Good Samaritan—Luke 10; the Two Great Commandments—Matthew 22:34–40; the Sermon on the Mount—Matthew 5–7; the Call of Abraham—Genesis 12; the Fall of Man—Genesis 3; the Golden Rule—Luke 6:31; the Parable of the Prodigal Son—Luke 15.

Chapter Fourteen
How Does God's Word Prepare Us for Spiritual Battle?

Possibly one of the great scenes in the history of television is a sequence run almost weekly on the "Wide World of Sports." As thrilling feats of athletic prowess flash on the television screen, the announcer drones on about how he and his camera crews are "spanning the globe to bring you the constant variety of sports—the thrill of victory—" At this moment the camera catches a fearless ski jumper hurtling down the incline. "—and the agony of defeat." Suddenly the jumper goes out of control, hurtles off the side of the jump before he even has a chance to become airborne, smashing through several signs and other apparatuses; and finally he cartwheels on down the slope to what seems certain death. (Fortunately, he was not hurt as badly as it appeared.)

We all identify with that jumper because we, too, have known the agony of defeat. I don't know about you, but I prefer to win. I don't like to lose. From the time I was old enough to lift a bat or a football or a schoolbook my dad taught me: "If you're going to do it, do it to the best of your ability, or don't do it at all."

I grew up trying to follow my dad's philosophy, always striving for excellence whenever I could. I don't like to be on the bottom. I prefer the top. And this philosophy carries over into my Christian life. I am not interested in beating fellow Christians (or non-Christians for that matter) at any cost, but I am interested in defeating Satan. I don't like to see Satan win anything. And I don't like to see the world master me. I don't like to see the flesh override the Spirit. When it comes to the world, the flesh, and the devil, I like to win as many rounds as possible.

We used to have a football coach who would give us the classic Knute Rockne lecture at halftime. One of his favorite sayings was, "You can't be beat if you won't be beat." I think Christians could use a motto like that as they go into daily spiritual combat. According to the Scriptures, we have the necessary equipment to gain victory. In fact, we have the ultimate weapon—the sword of the Spirit. All we need is the will to win.

The Most Important Piece of Armor

Most Christians are familiar with the "spiritual armor" passage in Ephesians 6. In Paul's analogy, written while he was chained to a Roman soldier, Paul describes equipment that is vital, not optional. The daily battle with Satan, not to mention the world and the flesh, is real, as anyone who has been a believer can tell you. Each piece of the Christian's armor is worth at least one chapter in any book, but here we are concentrating on that final item—the sword of the Spirit, God's authoritative Word.

To fully understand Paul's concept of the sword, we need to take a brief look at Greek terms. Paul does not use the Greek word for sword, *romphaia*, which stood for a huge weapon with a blade of forty inches or more. The *romphaia* was the great broad two-edged sword soldiers would wield with two hands. With a *romphaia*, a soldier wasn't interested in precision work. He flailed away with abandon and hoped he hit someone.

Instead, Paul uses a very common Greek word, *machaira*, which describes a weapon that could be anything from a six-inch dagger to a short eighteen-inch sword, a weapon easily wielded in combat to make defensive parries and attacking thrusts. The *machaira* was the kind of sword carried by most Roman soldiers in hand-to-hand combat.[1]

This word *machaira* is used in Matthew 26:47 to describe the weapons in the hands of the soldiers who came to arrest Jesus in the Garden of Gethsemane. It is the same word used for Peter's sword, the one used to slice off the ear of the high priest's servant. A *machaira* was for precise work. If Peter had used a *romphaia*, the poor fellow would have probably ended up in two pieces.

Note that Paul calls it the sword *of the Spirit*. I believe that he is basically referring to where the sword comes *from*—in this case *from* the Holy Spirit. There is a crucial difference between possessing the sword of the Spirit and simply possessing the Bible. An unbeliever can possess a Bible, but it does him little good. The natural man does not understand the things of God. But when we believe in Christ we receive the resident truth-teacher—the Holy Spirit. It is the Spirit of God in the life of the believer who makes the Word of God available and effective in the believer's life. Every Christian possesses the sword of the Spirit. How well he or she knows how to use it is the question.

But Ephesians 6:17 has still more to tell us. Paul says we need the sword of the Spirit, *the Word of God*. We have already seen that Paul was thinking of the *machaira* kind of sword, small and easily used for accurate cuts. He does not mention the *romphaia*, the huge broad sword that required two hands and mighty unguided swings. The Greek that Paul uses here for "word" is not *logos*, the standard definition for God's general revelation of Himself. Instead he uses the word *rema* which refers to "specific statements."

The principle Paul is clearly presenting in Ephesians 6:17 is when using the sword of the Spirit, we need to be specific. When temptation comes we cannot simply wave the Bible in the air and say, "God's Word will protect me!" We need to know which part of God's Word fits the situation. We need to know how to use the sword of the Spirit in our defense and on offense.

How's Your Defense?

If you have ever watched a sword fight you know that a sword is used as much to parry (turn aside) a blow as it is to deliver one. Without an adequate defense, the swordsman would quickly be cut down. The same principle applies to using God's Word in spiritual warfare. The Christian's first responsibility is to learn to use the sword of the Spirit with defensive skill. Satan attacks with constant temptations, but you can literally parry his blows with the proper use of God's Word.

Jesus gives His classic lesson in defensive strategy in the account of how He was tempted by Satan in three ways (see Matt. 4; Luke 4). It's worth noting that the temptations came to Jesus right after a moment of spiritual triumph. At His baptism by John, the Spirit of God descends on Him like a dove, and His Father's voice is heard saying, "This is My beloved Son, in whom I am well pleased" (Matt. 3:17). And in the next sentence we see Jesus in the wilderness, being tempted by the devil. The same thing can happen to any believer. When we experience a spiritual victory, we can be misled into thinking Satan can't touch us ever again. What seems like victory can quickly turn to defeat. Every moment brings new challenge. The battle never ceases.

Satan's first temptation of Jesus was simple. After fasting forty days and nights, Jesus was obviously hungry. "If You are the Son of God," said Satan, "command that these stones become bread" (see Matt. 4:3). Jesus looked at the thousands of rounded stones lying at His feet, each one looking like the rounded loaves baked in Palestinian ovens.[2] Was this simply an invitation to indulge His ravenous appetite? Surely the heavenly Father might forgive that, under the circumstances. But there is much more at stake here. The first word Satan uses is "if." *If* Jesus is the Son of God, surely He can do as He pleases. Surely God's Son should not have to starve. Satan is saying: "You're God's Son, so satisfy yourself. Why wander around out here any longer, unhonored, unattended, and starving? Is this befitting the Son of God? Use your power and authority and set things right!"

Jesus recognizes the temptation for what it is: an invitation to stop trusting in God and a temptation to use His own power and authority to satisfy His own wants. Jesus' answer is brief, precise, and straight from an Old Testament passage in Deuteronomy: "Man shall not live by bread alone, but by every word that proceeds from the mouth of God" (Matt. 4:4; see Deut. 8:3). Satan's first blow is parried, but Satan is merely warming up. The devil tries to beat Jesus at his own game, by quoting Scripture (a fact every Christian should keep in mind). Thus Satan's next suggestion is that Jesus cast Himself off the roof of the Temple, a fall of more than three hundred feet. After all, the angels will catch Him, just as it says in Psalm 91. Again, Jesus' answer is right on target and from the Scriptures: "It is written again: 'You shall not tempt the LORD your God' " (Matt. 4:7). In this case Satan was not only tempting Jesus to put on a show in order to attract followers, he was also tempting Jesus to see how far He could go with God the Father. God expects us to take risks in order to be true to Him but not take risks to enhance our own prestige.

Two of Satan's thrusts have been stopped cold, but he is still swinging. With his next offer he pulls out all the stops. Jesus can have all the kingdoms of the world, if He will just bow down and worship the devil. All He really would have to do is "compromise a little" and play the game. Relate to the worldly system a little more; be relevant and contemporary, instead of straight and old-fashioned. But Jesus wields the *machaira* again and quotes for the third time from Deuteronomy: "Away with you, Satan! For it is written: 'You shall worship the LORD your God, and Him only you shall serve' " (Matt. 4:10; see Deut. 6:13).

Jesus is so fed up with Satan's ploys that He tells him to get out of there; and Satan leaves. Three times the devil gives Jesus his best swing; and three times the devil fails. Why does Satan fail? It is because Jesus uses the sword of the Spirit in the precise way the temptation called for it to be used. Since all three of Jesus' answers came from Deuteronomy, we might wonder if that's the only book He knew. Hardly. He used Deuteronomy three times in a row, *because it fit each situation.* He could have just as easily quoted Psalms, Proverbs, Genesis—whatever passage fit.

The principle is very clear. When defending yourself from Satan's attacks, use the *machaira* of the Spirit, the *rema* of God, to specifically avoid each blow. The Christian has to be able to defend himself at whatever point the temptation appears. He has to have the principles, the passages, and the truths of God's Word in his heart and mind. He can't always take time to stop and ask the pastor at the church door or to dial a prayer. If the Christian can't parry the blow himself, Satan will score, and the Christian will lose that round.

Never doubt it for a minute—Satan has a way of knowing where you're weak, You may be able to fake it in a Bible study discussion or even with a Jehovah's Witness at your door, but you don't fool Satan. He will attack at your weakest point. You can never know enough of how to use the sword of the Spirit. It is all too easy to fall to temptation simply because you don't know how God's Word deals with the questions and problems that come at you every day.

Don't Forget to Go On the Offense

As much as I use God's Word to defend myself against Satan's attacks, I love to use it as an offensive weapon. That's when it's exciting. Staying on the defensive all the time gets old, but when I start using my sword of the Spirit in offense situations I see myself whacking away at some of the jungle of Satan's kingdom.

How do you use God's Word on offense? Every time you take the gospel to an unsaved person, the sword of the Spirit cuts a swath through Satan's kingdom of darkness. Every time you teach, or share, the Word in your family, in a class, among your friends, or on the job, you are slashing away at the undergrowth Satan uses to trap his prey.

Satan knows God's Word is effective, and that's why he tries to stop it whenever he can. In Luke 8, God's Word is compared to a seed, which Satan does his best to take away or choke out with weeds.

In spite of Satan's schemes, God's Word remains quick and powerful, so sharp it cuts us wide open to reveal our real motives (see Heb. 4:12). In Jeremiah 23:29 God asks: "Is not my word like fire? . . . And like a hammer that breaks a rock in pieces?" Who can forget Paul's bold, offensive statement in Romans 1:16: "I am not ashamed of the gospel of Christ, for it is the power of God to salvation for everyone who believes."

Using the sword of the Spirit on the offense is the same as using it for the defense. You have to make specific moves and precise thrusts. Have you gotten into a conversation and couldn't come up with answers because you didn't know what the Bible teaches in that area? That doesn't mean we should take refuge behind the "silent curtain." Better to admit you don't know. Then go find out. Look the question up in commentaries or study Bibles, such as the *MacArthur Study Bible*, so you can wield your sword more precisely and effectively the next time. The more we know the Word, the better we can march through Satan's kingdom cutting right through his core of lies.

Are You a Butterfly, Botanist, or Bee?

One of the common excuses Christians often give for not knowing the Word better than they do is that they "don't understand it." I don't buy that. God not only gave us His Word, He planted His resident truth-teacher—the Holy Spirit—in our hearts. He will teach us if we want to learn. G. Campbell Morgan, a pulpit giant of the last century, was approached by a man after preaching a stirring sermon. The man blurted, "Dr. Morgan, your preaching is such an inspiration!" Morgan is reported to have replied: "Ninety-five percent of inspiration is perspiration." That's right. It takes work to master the Bible, work done with skill and accuracy. Our sword of the Spirit is a *machaira,* not a *romphaia.*

An old but graphic illustration tells of a man who looked out of his window at a beautiful garden full of plants and flowers. First he saw a lovely butterfly, which would flutter from flower to flower, pausing for only a second or two before moving on. It touched many of the lovely blossoms but derived no benefit from them.

Next he spotted a botanist, with a big notebook under his arm and a large magnifying glass in his hand. The botanist would hunch over one flower for a long time, peering at it through his magnifying glass and scribbling furiously in his notebook. He stayed for hours, studying flowers and writing notes. Finally he closed his notebook, put his magnifying glass in his pocket and walked away.

The third visitor to the flower garden was a tiny bee. The bee would settle on a flower and sink down deep, extracting all the nectar it could carry. On each visit to a flower it went in empty and came out full.

So it is with Christians in their approach to God's Word. There are the butterflies who move from stirring sermon to stirring sermon, from Bible class to Bible class, fluttering here, fluttering there, gaining nothing but a nice feeling. Then there are the spiritual botanists who take copious notes. They are trying to get everything straight—from each vowel point to each point in the outline. They go over the words but don't draw much out of the flowers. It's all pure academics.

And then there are the people who are like spiritual bees. They sink down deep into every flower, every book or page of Scripture they come upon, and draw out the wisdom, truth, and life that is a blessing not only to them but to those around them.[3]

Which one are you? It's easy to spot the trouble with the butterfly, but the botanist's problem is more subtle. After all, isn't careful study of the Word what it's all about? Careful study of God's Word should go beyond your head and sink into your heart. The difference is obedience to the Holy Spirit, your resident truth-teacher, who can give you full benefit from God's Word if you give the Spirit free rein. You will come in and go out full—again and again and again. You will know how to use your sword of the Spirit, on defense, on offense, and in any way you need. Then in the daily spiritual battle, you will have your fair share of the thrill of victory.

To Sum It Up

Every Christian possesses the equipment necessary to gain victory in the daily struggle against the world, the flesh, and the devil. The crucial weapon is the sword of the Spirit, the Word of God, which is likened to a small, easily wielded weapon used for close, precision work. This sword is given by the Holy Spirit, who is the resident truth-teacher in every Christian's heart. It is the Word of God, which must be used specifically and precisely to be effective in the believer's life.

The two uses of the sword of the Spirit are defensive and offensive. On defense, we must learn to use the Word to parry the blows and thrusts of Satan, who is always trying to tempt us at our weakest point. On offense, we must be just as specific and precise as we wield the sword by teaching and sharing God's Word wherever we can to cut a swathe through the devil's dark kingdom.

There are three approaches to God's Word which can be likened to three visitors to a beautiful flower garden. We can be butterflies who flutter about, obtaining little of real value, or we can be botanists who carefully study the details and the fine points of the flower but who fail to find any real nourishment. Or we can be bees, who sink deep into God's Word, going in empty and coming out full of His truth, wisdom, and power.

How we choose to use our sword of the Spirit determines whether we will know the thrill of victory or the agony of defeat.

Chapter Fifteen
How Is the Bible Organized?

The Bible is a unique book. It is a collection of sixty-six documents inspired by God. These documents are gathered into two testaments, thirty-nine in the Old Testament and twenty-seven in the New Testament. Prophets, priests, kings, and leaders from the nation of Israel wrote the Old Testament books in Hebrew (with two passages in Aramaic). The apostles and their associates wrote the New Testament books in Greek.

The Old Testament record starts with the creation of the universe and closes about four hundred years before the birth of Jesus Christ.

The flow of history through the Old Testament moves along the following lines:

Creation of the universe
Fall of man
Flood over the earth
Abraham, Isaac, Jacob (Israel)—fathers of the chosen nation
The History of Israel

Exile in Egypt	430 years
Exodus and wilderness wanderings	40 years
Conquest of Canaan	7 years
Era of Judges	350 years
United Kingdom—Saul, David, Solomon	110 years
Divided Kingdom—Judah and Israel	350 years
Exile in Babylon	70 years
Return and rebuilding of the land	140 years

The details of this history are explained in the thirty-nine books divided into five different categories:

The Law	5 books (Genesis–Deuteronomy)
History	12 books (Joshua–Esther)
Wisdom	5 books (Job–Song Of Solomon)
Major Prophets	5 books (Isaiah–Daniel)
Minor Prophets	12 books (Hosea–Malachi)

After the completion of the Old Testament, there were four hundred years of silence, during which God did not speak, or inspire, any Scripture. That silence was broken by the arrival of John the Baptist announcing that the promised Savior had come. The New Testament records the rest of the story from the birth of Christ to the culmination of all history and the final eternal state; so the two testaments go from creation to consummation, eternity past to eternity future.

While the thirty-nine Old Testament books major on the history of Israel and the promise of the coming Savior, the twenty-nine New Testament books major on the person of Christ and the establishment of the church. The four Gospels give the record of His birth, life, death, resurrection, and ascension. Each of the four writers views the greatest and most important event of history, the coming of the God-man, Jesus Christ, from a different perspective. Matthew looks at Him through the perspective of His kingdom; Mark through the perspective of His servanthood; Luke through the perspective of His humanity; and John through the perspective of His deity.

The Book of Acts tells the story of the impact of the life, death, and resurrection of Jesus Christ—from His ascension, the consequent coming of the Holy Spirit, and the birth of the church, through the early years of gospel preaching by the apostles and their associates. Acts records the establishment of the church in Judea, Samaria, and throughout the Roman Empire.

The twenty-one epistles were written to churches and individuals to explain the significance of the person and work of Jesus Christ, with its implications for life and witness until He returns.

The New Testament closes with Revelation, which starts by picturing the current church age and culminates with Christ's return to establish His earthly kingdom, bringing judgment on the ungodly and glory and blessing for believers. Following the millennial reign of the Savior will be the last judgment, leading to the eternal state. All believers of all history finally enter the eternal glory prepared for them; and all the ungodly are consigned to hell to be punished forever.

The Five Themes of the Bible

To understand the Bible, it is essential to grasp the sweep of that history from creation to consummation. It is also crucial to keep in focus the unifying theme of Scripture. The one constant theme unfolding throughout the whole Bible is this: God for His own glory has chosen to create and gather to Himself a group of people to be the subjects of His eternal kingdom; to praise, honor, and serve Him forever; and through whom He will display His wisdom, power, mercy, grace, and glory. To gather His chosen ones, God must redeem them from sin. The Bible reveals God's plan for this redemption from its inception in eternity past to its completion in eternity future. Covenants, promises, and epochs are all secondary to the one continuous plan of redemption.

There is one God. The Bible has one Creator. It is one book. It has one plan of grace, recorded from initiation, through execution, to consummation. From predestination to glorification, the Bible is the story of God redeeming His chosen people for the praise of His glory.

As God's redemptive purpose and plan unfolds in Scripture, five recurring motifs are constantly emphasized:

(1) the nature of God
(2) the curse for sin and disobedience

(3) the blessing for faith and obedience
(4) the Lord Savior and the sacrifice for sin
(5) the coming kingdom and glory

Everything revealed on the pages of both the Old Testament and New Testament is associated with those five categories. Scripture is always teaching or illustrating: (1) the character and attributes of God; (2) the tragedy of sin and disobedience to God's holy standard; (3) the blessedness of faith and obedience to God's standard; (4) the need for a Savior by whose righteousness and substitution sinners can be forgiven, declared just, and transformed to obey God's standard; and (5) the coming glorious end of redemptive history in the Lord Savior's earthly kingdom and the subsequent eternal reign and glory of God and Christ. It is essential as one studies Scripture to grasp these recurring categories like great hooks on which to hang the passages. While reading through the Bible, one should be able to relate each portion of Scripture to these dominant topics, recognizing that what is introduced in the Old Testament is also made more clear in the New Testament. Looking at the five categories separately gives an overview of the Bible:

The Revelation of the Character of God

Above all else, Scripture is God's self-revelation. He reveals Himself as the Sovereign God of the universe who has chosen to make man and to make Himself known to man. In that self-revelation is established His standard of absolute holiness. From Adam and Eve through Cain and Abel and to everyone before and after the law of Moses, the standard of righteousness was established and is sustained to the last page of the New Testament. Violation of it produces judgment, temporal and eternal.

In the Old Testament record, God revealed Himself by the following means:

(1) creation—primarily through man—who was made in God's image
(2) angels
(3) signs, wonders, and miracles
(4) visions
(5) the words spoken by prophets and others
(6) written Scripture (Old Testament)

In the New Testament record, God revealed Himself again by the same means, but more clearly and fully.

(1) creation—the God-man, Jesus Christ, who was the very image of God
(2) angels
(3) signs, wonders, and miracles
(4) visions
(5) spoken words by apostles and prophets
(6) written Scripture (New Testament)

The Revelation of Divine Judgment for Sin and Disobedience

Scripture repeatedly deals with the matter of man's sin, which leads to divine judgment. Account after account in Scripture demonstrates the deadly effects in time and eternity of violating God's standard. There are 1,189 chapters in the Bible. Only four of them don't involve a fallen world: the first two and the last two—before the fall and after the creation of the new heaven and new earth. The rest is a chronicle of the tragedy of sin.

In the Old Testament, God showed the disaster of sin—starting with Adam and Eve to Cain and Abel, the patriarchs, Moses and Israel, the kings, priests, some prophets, and Gentile nations. Throughout the Old Testament is the relentless record of continual devastation produced by sin and disobedience to God's law.

In the New Testament, the tragedy of sin becomes more clear. The preaching and teaching of Jesus and the apostles begin and end with a call to repentance. King Herod, the Jewish leaders, and the nation of Israel—along with Pilate, Rome, and the rest of the world—all reject the Lord Savior, spurn the truth of God, and thus condemn themselves. The chronicle of sin continues unabated to the end of the age and the return of Christ in judgment. In the New Testament, disobedience is even more flagrant than Old Testament disobedience because it involves the rejection of the Lord Savior Jesus Christ in the brighter light of New Testament truth.

The Revelation of Divine Blessing for Faith and Obedience

Scripture repeatedly promises wonderful rewards in time and eternity that come to people who trust God and seek to obey Him. In the Old Testament, God showed the blessedness of repentance from sin, faith in Himself, and obedience to His Word—from Abel, through the patriarchs, to the remnant in Israel—and even to the Gentiles who believed (such as the people of Nineveh).

God's standard for man, His will, and His moral law was always made known. To those who faced their inability to keep God's standard, recognized their sin, confessed their impotence to please God by their own effort and works, and asked Him for forgiveness and grace—there came merciful redemption and blessing for time and eternity.

In the New Testament, God again showed the full blessedness of redemption from sin for repentant people. There were those who responded to the preaching of repentance by John the Baptist. Others repented at the preaching of Jesus. Still other Jews obeyed the gospel through the apostles' preaching. And finally, there were Gentiles all over the Roman Empire who believed the gospel. To all those and to all who will believe through all of history, there is blessing promised in this world and the world to come.

The Revelation of the Lord Savior and the Sacrifice for Sin

Jesus as Savior is the heart of both the Old Testament, which Jesus said spoke of Him in type and prophecy, and the New Testament, which gives the biblical record of His coming. The promise of blessing is dependent on grace and mercy given to the sinner. Grace means that sin is not held against the sinner. Such forgiveness is dependent on a payment of sin's penalty to satisfy holy justice. That requires a substitute—one to die in the sinners' place. God's chosen substitute—the only one who qualified—was Jesus.

Salvation is always by the same gracious means, whether during Old or New Testament times. When any sinner comes to God, repentant and convinced he has no power to save himself from the deserved judgment of God, and pleads for mercy, God's promise of forgiveness is granted. God then declares him righteous because the sacrifice and obedience of Christ is put to his account. In the Old Testament, God justified sinners that same way, in anticipation of Christ's atoning work. There is, therefore, a continuity of grace and salvation through all of redemptive history. Various covenants, promises, and epochs do not alter that fundamental continuity neither does the discontinuity between the Old Testament witness—the nation of Israel—and the New Testament witness—the church. A fundamental continuity is centered in the Cross. The Cross was no interruption in the plan of God but the very event to which all else points.

Throughout the Old Testament, the Savior and sacrifice is promised. In Genesis, Jesus is the Seed of the woman and the One who will destroy Satan (Gen. 3:15). In Zechariah, He is the pierced one to whom Israel turns and by whom God opens the fountain of forgiveness to all who mourn over their sin (Zech. 12:10). He is the very One symbolized in the sacrificial system of the Mosaic law. He is the suffering substitute spoken of by the prophets (Is. 53:3, 4, 11). Throughout the Old Testament, He is the Messiah who would die for the transgressions of His people; from beginning to end in the Old Testament, the theme of the Lord Savior and sacrifice for sin is presented. It is solely because of His perfect sacrifice for sin that God graciously forgives repentant believers.

In the New Testament, the Lord Savior came and actually provided the promised sacrifice for sin on the Cross. Having fulfilled all righteousness by His perfect life, He fulfilled justice by His death. Thus God Himself atoned for sin, at a cost too great for the human mind to fathom. Now He graciously supplies on His people's behalf all the merit necessary for them to be the objects of His favor. That is what Scripture means when it speaks of salvation by grace.

The Revelation of the Kingdom and Glory of the Lord Savior

This crucial component of Scripture brings the whole story to its God-ordained consummation. Redemptive history is controlled by God, so as to culminate in His eternal glory. Redemptive history will end with the same precision and exactness with which it began. The truths of eschatology are neither vague nor unclear—neither are they unimportant. As in any book, how the story ends is the most crucial and compelling part—so with the Bible. Scripture notes several specific features of the end planned by God.

In the Old Testament, there is repeated mention of an earthly kingdom ruled by the Messiah, Lord Savior, who will come to reign. Associated with that kingdom will be the salvation of Israel, the salvation of the Gentiles, the renewal of the earth from the effects of the curse, and the bodily resurrection of God's people who have died. Finally, the Old Testament predicts that there will be the "uncreation" or dissolution of the universe, and the creation of a new heaven and a new earth (which will be the eternal state of the godly) and a final hell for the ungodly.

In the New Testament, these features are clarified and expanded. The King was rejected and executed, but He promised to come back in glory, bringing judgment, resurrection, and His kingdom for all who believe. Innumerable Gentiles from every nation will be included among the redeemed. Israel will be saved, grafted back into the root of blessing from which she has been temporarily excised.

Israel's promised kingdom will be enjoyed, with the Lord Savior reigning on the throne, in the renewed earth, exercising power over the whole world, having taken back His rightful authority and receiving due honor and worship. Following that kingdom will come the dissolution of the renewed, but still sin-stained creation, and the subsequent creation of a new heaven and new earth, which will be the eternal state, separate forever from the ungodly in hell.

To Sum It Up

Those are the five topics that fill up the Bible. To understand them at the start is to know the answer to the question that continually arises: Why does the Bible tell us this? Everything fits into this glorious pattern. As you read the Bible, hang the truth on these five hooks, and the Bible will unfold, not as sixty-six separate documents or even two separate testaments but as one book, by one divine Author, who wrote it all with one overarching theme.

My prayer is that the magnificent and overwhelming theme of the redemption of sinners for the glory of God will carry every reader with captivating interest from beginning to end of this story. This story is from God to you; and it is all about you. Read it. Study it with Bible study tools, such as this book, the *MacArthur Study Bible,* and various commentaries. It tells you what God has planned for you, why He made you, what you were, what you have become in Christ, and what He has prepared for you in eternal glory.

Chapter Sixteen
WHAT DOES THE BIBLE SAY?

If the previous chapters of this book have accomplished anything, they have demonstrated again and again that in the Bible all Christians have an incredible treasure. Effective study of the Word of God is basic to the Christian life. For the Christian, at the core of everything is knowledge of God's Word.

Prerequisites for Worthwhile Bible Study

If we want to know God through His Word it is vital to have the right attitude. Effective Bible study takes at least five things: new birth, real desire, constant diligence, practical holiness, and prayer.

New birth, being born again, seems obvious, but it is vital. In order to get anything out of God's Word, you have to belong to God. The natural man doesn't understand God's truths because he lacks the resident truth-teacher, the Holy Spirit (see 1 Cor. 2:14).

Real desire to know the Word is crucial. In recent years there has been a great deal of stress on emotionalism, on getting some kind of charge out of Christianity. But you shouldn't primarily come to the Bible for a feeling. The Scriptures are not a sanctified pep pill. The Scriptures are there to give you knowledge, and gaining that knowledge takes effort. The more you want to make that effort, the more you are going to gain from Scripture.

Halfhearted Bible study is a bore. If you come to the Scriptures legalistically, ritualistically, or because you're intimidated by your peers or your pastor, you won't get much out of it. What you need is a hunger in your heart, a passion for knowing God through His Word. Ask yourself how much do you really want to know God. Where is this "desire" on your priority list?

Constant diligence comes right on the heels of real desire. Your wants have to result in action; or nothing will happen. There is no avoiding it; studying the Bible is hard work. The Holy Spirit is not going to zap us as we stroll through the park or slouch in front of the television set. The Spirit works through the Word; and we have to work to get His message for us.

In addition to a myriad of duties as pastor of a large church I spend some twenty-five to thirty hours per week in sermon preparation. To be honest, there are days when I don't feel as diligent as I would like. The passion to know God burns at a lower ebb. It would be more fun to take the family to the beach, watch a ball game, or just relax at home with the paper and some favorite magazines. At times such as that I have to remember the Berean Christians in Acts 17. Luke calls them noble because they searched the Scriptures daily (see Acts 17:11). Second Timothy 2:15 tells me: "Be diligent to present yourself approved to God, a worker who does not need to be ashamed, rightly dividing the word of truth." Bible study takes discipline. If there is no perspiration, there will be no inspiration.

Practical holiness is a fourth prerequisite. I call it "practical" because I simply mean "having a cleaned-up life." I can talk about holiness in very spiritual and mysterious terms, but the bottom line is "How pure is my life?" The key to growth is *first* laying aside (stripping off) malice, deceit, hypocrisy, envy, and gossip and then going to the sincere milk of the Word to grow as Christians (see 1 Pet. 2:1, 2).

If you insist on practicing certain favorite sins, the sincere milk of the Word won't set all that well. You will wind up with indigestion or, more often than not, you will decide you are just not hungry.

Prayer is another crucial element of Bible study. The early apostles reduced their priorities to two: "We will give ourselves continually to prayer and to the ministry of the word" (Acts 6:4). Scripture study and prayer go together. Prayer is seeking the divine Source of understanding—God Himself.

The apostle Paul underlined the centrality of prayer in gaining biblical understanding when he wrote: "[I] do not cease to give thanks for you, making mention of you in my prayers: that the God of our Lord Jesus Christ . . . may give to you the spirit of wisdom and revelation in the knowledge of Him, the eyes of your understanding being enlightened" (Eph. 1:16–18).

Paul sensed deeply the need for divine enlightenment through revelation from God, and he sought it through prayer. No Christian should ever look down at the Word without first looking up at the very Source of that Word and asking for guidance. To engage in Bible study without prayer is presumption, if not sacrilege.

Having looked over some of the prerequisites for worthwhile Bible study, let's move on to just how it's done. The first step is simple—perhaps too simple.

Read God's Word Systematically

The first step in Bible study is to *read the Bible.* I can't emphasize too strongly that effective Bible study has to begin with a systematic reading of the Scriptures. Other methods will be of limited benefit unless you get the entire flow and context of what God's Word is saying.

With all of the Bible study tools, methods, and resources on the market today, Christians are tempted to make the same mistakes as did the Jews of the southern kingdom of Judah when Isaiah prophesied their destruction at the hands of foreign invaders. They scoffed at Isaiah's warnings, as if they were mere Sunday School moralizing. They thought they were far above and beyond the principle that "precept must be upon precept, precept upon precept; line upon line, line upon line; here a little, and there a little" (Is. 28:10). Their end is well known. Judah fell to the Babylonians in 586 B.C. The scoffers who thought they were beyond the fundamentals and the basics were marched into captivity.[1]

The point is well made: no believer is ever beyond the basics. Sophisticated and ingenious Bible study methods and books are fine, but they should never come ahead of fundamental steps. And there is no more fundamental step than systematically reading God's Word, line upon line, precept upon precept, absorbing its total truth and cohesiveness.

A Plan for the Old Testament

Of course you need a plan for your reading. For the Old Testament, I suggest reading through all of it once a year in a narrative manner (from Genesis to Malachi, no skipping around). True, there are some difficult portions. The going is a bit heavy through Leviticus and parts of Deuteronomy, but by and large the Hebrew language of the Old Testament translates into very simple, concrete reading.

I have studied Hebrew and Greek; and the difference between them is significant. Greek is an intensely complex language and often difficult to interpret because of its philosophical nature. It has many abstract ways of saying things. Hebrew, on the other hand, is more concrete and simple.

Thus the best way to read the Old Testament is straight through, like a story. Don't look for a presentation of systematic theology. Don't start by looking for "types," allegories, and dispensations. You can do that later, after you get into Bible interpretation. First, simply read the Old Testament to see what it says, to hear the story it has to tell. You will see the unfolding of God's progressive revelation; and you will also discover foundations for New Testament truths that come later.

As you read, keep a pencil and notebook in hand. Jot down notes regarding areas you want to come back and study in depth later. When you come to a passage you don't understand completely, don't let it bog you down. Put a question mark in the margin and move on. As you continue to read the Old Testament year by year, line upon line and precept upon precept, you will begin to erase the question marks.

What is the best way to organize your reading of the Old Testament? How many chapters per day, per week?

One simple plan is this. There are 929 chapters in the entire Old Testament. Divide 929 by 365 days and you come up with merely two-and-a-half chapters a day. To allow for occasional days when you may miss due to illness or other problems, set a goal of at least three chapters a day, which should take an average of 15 to 20 minutes. Keep in mind that some chapters are quite long, others are very short. The average chapter usually occupies about a page in a typical Bible, so the goal of three chapters a day is definitely not overwhelming.[2]

A Plan for the New Testament

With the New Testament, I use a little different approach. I still keep the principle of repetition from Isaiah 28:9 (line upon line, precept upon precept) but with an important variation. Instead of reading through the entire New Testament from Matthew to Revelation, I read each book over and over for thirty days. This works beautifully with the shorter books, for example 1 John. In fact I started using this system with 1 John. I read it straight through in one sitting. It took about thirty minutes. Perhaps you have never read an entire book all the way through, even a short one. But reading a book straight through in one sitting gives you the context and flow. It helps get you off the "proof-text and memory-verse" syndrome. Memorization of the Bible is important, but unless it's done with an organized approach, such as the one used by the Navigators,[3] it's too easy to get the idea that the Bible is a collection of important sayings.

The Bible has a flow and a context, especially the letters from Paul, James, and others. When somebody writes you a letter, you don't stop to read a nice line, then jump two pages to find another good thought. You read it through, to understand the flow of thought.

So, sit down and read 1 John through. Are you through? Hardly. The next day read 1 John through in one sitting again. On the third day, do it again and so on for thirty days. Do you know what happens at the end of thirty days? You know what is in 1 John. Nobody can trip you up. Where does it talk about forgiveness of sins? 1 John 1:7–9. Where does John talk about how and why God is love? 1 John 4:7–21. For warnings about loving the world too much see 1 John 2:15–17. For the promise of eternal life, see 1 John 5:11, 12.

Those are just a few obvious samples. You'll be able to see 1 John in your mind's eye—the location of every verse, where every line fits. Best of all, you will have the flow of the book and understand its basic message. Then go on to another short book and do the same thing for thirty days. Always read the book through in one sitting, every day, for thirty days. At the end of thirty days, you'll have another New Testament book in your heart and mind as never before.

You might be thinking that this is fine for shorter books like 1 John, Colossians, or Philippians, but what about longer books like Matthew, John, or Acts?

There's an easy answer to that problem. You break the longer books up and still use the same thirty-day system. For example, the Gospel of John has twenty-one chapters. Divide it into three sections of seven chapters each. Read the first seven chapters daily for thirty days. Then take the next seven and read them daily for thirty days, and likewise with the last seven. In ninety days you will cover the Gospel of John with your own custom-made, fine-tooth, reading comb. And I guarantee you will know what's in there. Jesus and Nicodemus? John 3. The first miracle at the wedding in Cana? John 2. The calling of the disciples? John 1. The chapter on the vine and the branches? John 15. The Good Shepherd? John 10. The Bread of Life discourse? John 6.

If you want to know what the Bible says, this method will let you find out like no other. Vary the length of the books you tackle. First a short one, then a long one, then back to a couple of short ones. In two-and-a-half years you will cover the entire New Testament thirty times, and somewhere along the way it will all start to come together as never before. A truth in Colossians will match up with one in Ephesians. Paul's arguments in Romans will correspond with his polemics in Galatians. The parable of the Good Samaritan will dovetail with the practical instructions in Romans 12, Ephesians 5, and Galatians 6.

Of course you might be saying, "Oh, this is too hard. I can't possibly keep up a schedule like that. It's easy for John MacArthur; he has to do this thirty hours a week to prepare his sermons."

There are several answers to this problem. First, this thirty-minutes-a-day-for-thirty-days approach is worth the effort. It will free you from the bewilderment many Christians experience when they pick up the Bible. Many unconsciously say, "Oh, look at all this. I can't possibly absorb all this, or make much sense out of it. I'll let the pastor sort it out, and feed it to me in bite-size pieces." Those type of Christians stay that way, being spoon fed, instead of really knowing the Word for themselves.

Yes, it will take discipline. You may even get bored. For some people the boredom comes at the seventh day, the twelfth day, or the nineteenth. Part of the reason for this is that you will still be reading the Bible as you always have—somewhat superficially. The way to fight boredom is to look deeper into what you're reading. Begin to really search out what the writer is saying. Read slower, not faster. Soon you will find yourself saying, "Oh, I see!" "Ah, this makes sense." "Now I get it."

Yes, you may have days when you don't pull it off. You may miss your reading due to illness, emergencies, traveling, and other responsibilities. The system, however, is what counts. As best you can, *stick to the system*. Read each book, or portion, all the way through as often as you can on a daily basis. But be flexible. On some days perhaps you should spend more time at prayer. Let the Holy Spirit guide you in developing a personal Bible reading system that works best for you.

One other point. If you want to get serious about Bible reading and study you will have to reset your priorities. All of us have to fight laziness and inertia. To do anything worthwhile you have to pay a price. As a student in seminary I heard leading scholars and students of the Bible explain how to study the Bible. They all virtually said the same thing: read the Scriptures repetitiously.

Your first goal is to find out what the Bible says. The second step is finding out what it means. We'll discuss that in the next chapter. That is when Bible study tools, such as commentaries, Bible dictionaries, and study Bibles, like the *MacArthur Study Bible*, become useful to your study of God's Word.

To Sum It Up

To know God—really know Him—through His Word is a vital goal for every Christian. To know God so that He actually speaks to us through His biblical message takes regular, effective Bible study. To make study of the Bible worthwhile, we need: the new birth, a real desire to learn, constant diligence, practical holiness, and prayer.

The first step in worthwhile Bible study is to read the Bible. That may seem too obvious and simple. But unless we are reading the Bible regularly and systematically, we will learn little. Bible study tools and resources have their place, but they should never replace reading the Scriptures over and over, line upon line, precept upon precept.

A good plan for reading the Old Testament is to read it straight through. This way you cover its entire story of progressive revelation. With the New Testament, a good plan to cover its new covenant truths is to read the same book every day for thirty days to get its flow and become completely familiar with its truths. With larger New Testament books, divide them into sections and cover each section each day for thirty days. For example, you can cover the twenty-one chapters in the Gospel of John, by doing seven chapters for thirty days, then seven more for another thirty days, and the last seven over another thirty days.

Is the read-a-book-daily-for-thirty-days system too difficult? While you might miss a day now and then, it is well worth the effort. In two-and-a-half years, you will know God's Word as you never did before.

Chapter Seventeen
What Does the Bible Mean?

A young couple from another church came to one of our assistant pastors for counseling about marital problems they started having soon after their wedding. After just a few minutes of interviewing the two, he could see they were miles apart in tastes, ideas, and opinions.

"What made the two of you get married?" he asked.

"A sermon our pastor preached on Joshua conquering Jericho."

"What did that have to do with getting married?"

"Well," explained the husband, "Joshua and his army claimed Jericho, marched around it seven times, and the walls fell down. Our pastor told us that if we trusted God, claimed a certain young girl and marched around her seven times, the walls of her heart would collapse, and she would be willing to marry. So, I did it, and we got married."

Our assistant pastor stared in disbelief. Was this man putting him on? No, indeed. In fact, several couples in that particular church had gotten married on the same basis after hearing the same sermon.

This amazing story illustrates that first of all people can become extremely confused on what the Bible means and what to do about it; and second the interpretation and application of Scripture is crucial to life decisions.

The Importance of Cutting It Straight

The interpretation of Scripture has been something of a battleground for centuries for an obvious reason: it seems so subjective. Doesn't everyone have his own view? Isn't one view as valid as another? Not necessarily. I believe there are sound principles for scriptural interpretation. There are some difficult areas. That's true. There are some issues we'll never all agree on because our information is incomplete. As Deuteronomy 29:29 so wisely says: "The secret things belong to the LORD our God."

On the other hand there is an awful lot in God's Word that we can interpret in a sound and orderly manner. As Mark Twain, the agnostic, admitted: "It's not the things I don't understand in the Bible that bother me. It's the things I do understand."

The apostle Paul would have agreed with Mark Twain at that point. When he wrote to Timothy, Paul said: "Be diligent to present yourself approved to God, a worker who does not need to be ashamed, rightly dividing the word of truth" (2 Tim. 2:15). The Greek for "rightly dividing" literally means "cutting it straight."

Paul had been a tentmaker, and he may well have used this phrase as he compared the making of tents with the study of Scripture. In Paul's time, tents were made in a patchwork design with animal skins. To get all the parts to fit properly, they had to be cut correctly. The same is true of Scripture. The Bible is a whole. God has given us the whole tent, so to speak. But if we don't cut straight on the individual pieces (the verses, chapters, and books), the whole won't fit together. We won't handle His Word correctly.

The result of "cutting it crooked" can be anything from minor errors to total chaos and confusion. An example of chaos is what cults do as they cut Scripture according to their own crooked patterns. But plenty of crooked cutting goes on in the ranks of biblical Christians, too. Incredible points have been proved with careless, or crooked, use of Scripture.

Theologians call the science of Bible interpretation *hermeneutics* (from the Greek word, *hermeneuo*). To escape faulty hermeneutics, we should avoid some basic errors.

Making a point at the price of proper interpretation is a common temptation for pastors who want to force the Scriptures to agree with their sermons; but lay people can fall into the same trap. A classic example is the rabbi who took the story of the Tower of Babel and claimed that it teaches us to be more concerned for one another. How did he come up with that? Because his research in the *Talmud* revealed that as the tower grew taller, workmen carrying loads of bricks to the bricklayers would fall and die. Those in charge of the project were distraught when a workman fell on the way up—and lost the load of bricks, too. But if a workman fell on the way down with an empty hod, it was no big deal. All the project coordinators lost was a workman.

The crass inhumanity of the tower builders carries a lesson, true. But it is not the lesson in the biblical account of the Tower of Babel, which teaches that God confused the languages of men because they rebelled against Him. God destroyed the Tower of Babel because it was a symbol of idolatry, not because the builders cared more about bricks than people.

In Bible study, get the right message from the right passage. Don't "proof text" your bias or opinions by making the Bible say what you already know you want it to say.

Spiritualizing, or allegorizing, Scripture is another gimmick ministers will use—in the pulpit or in their writings. We have already seen one funny, but tragic, example of allegory overkill with the how-to-get-a-mate message based on the biblical account of the fall of Jericho.

I heard another example of allegory that was out of control at a conference, where one of the speakers talked about John 11, the story of the resurrection of Lazarus. This was his interpretation: "Lazarus is a symbol of the church, and what we have here is a vivid picture of the rapture of the believers. The resurrection of Lazarus is the church going through the rapture."

Afterward, this speaker came up and said, "John, did you ever see that in the text before?" I tried to be honest but diplomatic: "You know, I doubt that anyone has ever seen that in the text before. You are the first."

There are passages in Scripture that are symbolic. There are passages that give us types and pictures. But beware of interpretations that read symbols and pictures into the text that simply are not there.

I call this "Little Bo Peep" preaching. You don't need the Bible. You can use Mother Goose, Aesop's Fables, or the Yellow Pages to prove your point. The "reasoning" flows like this: "Little Bo Peep has lost her sheep. What a tragedy to be lost. All over the world people are lost. Who can find them . . ." The spiritualizing of the text continues on and on into an allegorical swamp that makes the Slough of Despond look like a well-paved parking lot.

Putting It All Together Inductively

While it's helpful to know about some of the errors to avoid in Bible study, the key questions for many Christians are still: "How do I put it all together?" "How can I work out a Bible study method that will let me work at my own speed and at my own level of ability?"

If you have visited your Christian bookstore lately, you know there are hundreds of Bible study helps on the market. You can become swamped by just reading all the titles. After finally choosing a book, you can spend hours familiarizing yourself with the book's contents and still not study the Bible itself.

My solution is something you may have heard of—inductive Bible study. The word "inductive" means reasoning from the specific to the general, from the parts to the whole. It is the opposite of deductive reasoning, in which you move from the general to the specific.

There are several excellent inductive Bible study books, commentaries, and methods on the market. You may want to examine some of these various methods for yourself. But right here, let me give you a simple four-step approach that can get you going immediately in learning to "cut it straight."

Observation is the first step. Read the Bible text over and over. As you observe what is being said in the Bible, take notes. Here are some questions to keep in mind: Who was the writer? To whom was he writing? To what location and from what location was he writing? What was the situation or occasion? When did it occur? What historical or cultural factors might have a bearing on understanding the passage?

Keep in mind that there are several "gaps" you will have to hurdle: language, culture, history, and geography. If you have a good study Bible, such as the *MacArthur Study Bible* or *The Ryrie Study Bible,* many of the above questions are answered in an introduction printed at the beginning of each book.

Interpretation is the second step. When you interpret Scripture it is important to do your own work. There are certain study tools you can use, but don't resort to commentaries at this point. Dig in and determine what the passage means, as you go through the following steps:

(1) Underline key words and phrases and define them in terms of the context—what the passage is saying. Underline only the most basic and important words at first, then use your Bible dictionary, concordance, and word study book to study meanings.

(2) Paraphrase (put into your own words) each verse or section of the passage. If this grows laborious, try putting the basic thought conveyed in a passage or paragraph into one sentence. This may seem like a lot of work (and for some people it is), but it forces you to think over the meaning of the passage and put it into your own words, a process that is extremely beneficial.

(3) List the divine truths and principles in the verse, paragraph, or passage. Ask the following questions: (i) Is there a command God has given? (ii) Is there an example to follow? (iii) Is there some sin I should avoid? (iv) Is there a warning against false teaching of any kind? (v) Is there a basic doctrinal truth about God, Christ, the Holy Spirit, Satan, or man? (vi) Is there a promise from God to Christian believers, Israel, the church, or unbelievers? (Note the conditions of the promise, as for example in Matthew 6:33.)

(4) Cross reference as many truths, or principles, as possible. Do you find these same truths taught in other parts of Scripture? Use your concordance, or other Bible study tools, to discover these truths. List

at least one or two truths, but don't get bogged down with trying to list six or eight.

Evaluation is the third step. Here is where you stop to check what commentators and other scholars have said about the passage—from what I have said in the *MacArthur Study Bible* to what various biblical scholars have said in *The Nelson Study Bible.* You have already covered this to some extent in doing your observation and interpretation, but go back again to see what divine truths or principles are emphasized by the Bible commentaries and the study Bibles in your library. You may modify your own understandings or conclusions, but don't always think you have to agree with every commentator. Make them prove themselves. As somebody once said, "The Bible is a good commentary on the commentaries."

Application is the last step. How can the passage become relevant for your life? What does the Lord want you to stop doing? What does He want you to start doing? What should you be doing more often?

Keep in mind that application of Bible truth does not have to be a profound, life-or-death issue. You can apply God's Word right at home—every morning as you're getting ready for work or every evening during that crucial dinner hour when everybody's tired and hungry. You can apply it at church, in your neighborhood, on the job anywhere you have relationships with others. It might be interesting to keep tabs on how many applications of Scripture you actually make. Record them in your study notebook. How many do you have after a month? Three months? A year?

All of the other steps and principles in Bible study will be of little use unless we finally employ practical application. That's precisely what Paul was talking about when he told Timothy that all Scripture "is given by inspiration of God, and is profitable for doctrine, for reproof, for correction, for instruction in righteousness" (2 Tim. 3:16).

Biblical teaching, or doctrine, is basic. Here we have found out what Scripture says and means. But the final and crucial questions are: So what? What are you going to do about it? How do you use it in your own life?

That's where the rebuking, correcting, and training come in. As Scripture rebukes us, it reveals our sin and shows us how to and why we should change. Our next step is correcting our course, changing our path, developing new habits. It all adds up to being trained in the Word—disciples in whom the Word of Christ dwells richly as we give thanks to Him (see Col. 3:15–17).

To Sum It Up

Interpretation of Scripture can be a confusing battleground if sound objective principles are not employed. According to 2 Timothy 2:15 (consult the NKJV translation), the Christian is to learn to rightly divide the word of truth—"to cut it straight." Examples of cutting Scripture in a "crooked way"—misinterpreting it completely or partially—have been plentiful throughout history.

One basic error that befalls some Bible students is to try to make a point at the price of proper interpretation. In other words, don't proof text a biased opinion in order to make the Bible say what you want it to say.

Another basic error is spiritualizing or allegorizing Scripture. This "Little Bo Peep" approach allows the imagination to run wild in order to get a "meaning" from a biblical passage. When allegorical language is used in Scripture it is usually fairly obvious. Trouble starts when Bible teachers, preachers, and others start allegorizing biblical passages that don't have any allegories in them.

A basic Bible study method is the inductive approach. Key steps in the inductive approach include observation, interpretation, evaluation, and most important application. Scripture teaches, rebukes, corrects, and trains us (see 2 Tim. 3:16), as we let the word of Christ dwell in us richly (see Col. 3:15–17).

Notes

Chapter Two

1. For a more comprehensive look at this subject see my book, *The Charismatics* (Grand Rapids: Zondervan Publishing House), pp. 15–39.

Chapter Five

1. "The Chicago Statement on Biblical Inerrancy" finalized at a summit meeting of the International Council on Biblical Inerrancy, held in Chicago, Illinois in October, 1978. Chairman was James M. Boice. Council members were: Gleason L. Archer, James M. Boice, Edmund P. Clowney, Norman L. Geisler, John H. Gerstner, Jay H. Grimstead, Harold W. Hoehner, Donald E. Hoke, A. Wetherell Johnson, Kenneth S. Kantzer, James I. Packer, J. Barton Payne, Robert D. Preus, Earl D. Radmacher, Francis A. Schaeffer, R. C. Sproul.
2. Ibid.
3. Ibid.
4. D. Martyn Lloyd-Jones, "The Authority of the Scripture," *Eternity* (April, 1957).
5. Ibid.
6. Ibid.
7. Ibid.
8. Billy Graham, "The Authority of the Scriptures," *Decision* (June, 1963).

Chapter Six

1. John F. MacArthur, Jr., *Focus on Fact* (Old Tappan, N. J.: Fleming H. Revell Company, 1977); Henry Morris, *Many Infallible Proofs* (San Diego: Creation-Life Publishers, 1974); Batsell B. Baxter, *I Believe Because* (Grand Rapids: Baker Book House, 1971); Bernard Ramm, *Protestant Christian Evidences* (Chicago: Moody Press, 1953); Harold Lindsell, *God's Incomparable Word* (Wheaton: Victor Books, 1977); James C. Hefley, *Adventures with God . . . Scientists Who Are Christians* (Grand Rapids: Zondervan Publishing House, 1967).
2. Paraphrase of Augustine's words in *De Genesi ad Litteram* as quoted in Fritz Ridenour, *Who Says?* (Glendale, Calif.: Regal Books, 1967), p. 151.

3. W. F. Albright, *Archaeology and the Religion of Israel* (Baltimore: Johns Hopkins Press, 1956).
4. Fritz Ridenour, *Who Says?* (Glendale, Calif.: Regal Books, 1967), pp. 84, 85.
5. Ibid., p. 85.
6. See, for example, Miller Burrows, *What Mean These Stones?* (American School of Royal Research, 1977); Donald J. Weisman and Edwin Yamauchi, *Archaeology and the Bible: An Introductory Study* (Grand Rapids: Zondervan Publishing House, 1979); Clifford A. Wilson, *Rocks, Relics and Biblical Reliability* (Grand Rapids: Zondervan Publishing House, 1977).
7. Ridenour, *Who Says?* pp. 78, 79.

CHAPTER SEVEN

1. D. Martyn Lloyd-Jones, *Authority* (Downers Grove, Ill.: InterVarsity, 1958), p. 17.
2. Ibid., p. 19.
3. Robert P. Lightner, *The Saviour and the Scriptures* (Nutley, N. J.: Presbyterian and Reformed Publishing Co., 1973), p. 83.
4. F. F. Bruce, *The Books and the Parchments* (London: Pickering and Inglis, 1950), p. 164.
5. R. T. France, *Jesus and the Old Testament* (Wheaton, Ill.: Tyndale House Publishers, 1971), p. 27.
6. James I. Packer, *Fundamentalism and the Word of God* (Grand Rapids: Wm. B. Eerdmans Publishing Co., 1958), pp. 54–62.
7. Norman L. Geisler and William E. Nix, *A General Introduction to the Bible* (Chicago: Moody Press, 1968), pp. 59, 60.
8. John M. M'Clintock and James Strong, "Accommodation," *Cyclopaedia of Biblical, Theological-Ecclesiastical Literature* Vol. l. (New York: Arno Press, 1969), p. 47.
9. Milton S. Terry, *Biblical Hermeneutics* (Grand Rapids: Zondervan, 1974), p. 166.
10. Geisler and Nix, *General Introduction*, p. 60.
11. Ibid., p. 61.
12. Lightner, *The Saviour and the Scriptures*, p. 47.
13. Packer, *Fundamentalism*, p. 61.
14. For a good discussion of Jesus' promise of divine inspiration to the authors of the New Testament, see René Pache, *The Inspiration and Authority of Scripture* (Chicago: Moody Press, 1969), pp. 90, 91.

CHAPTER EIGHT

1. Henry M. Morris, *Many Infallible Proofs* (San Diego: Creation-Life Publishers, 1974), p. 157.
2. Ibid., p. 159.

3. G. Abbot-Smith, *Manual Greek Lexicon of the New Testament* (Edinburgh: T. and T. Clark, 1921), p. 230.
4. Merrill C. Tenney, *The New Testament* (Grand Rapids: Wm. Eerdmans Publishing Co., 1953), p. 47.
5. B. F. Wescot, *A General Survey of the History of the Canon of the New Testament* (London: Macmillan Publishing Company, 1875), p. 516.
6. For a full discussion of the development of the Old Testament canon, Norman L. Geisler and William E. Nix, *From God to Us: How We Got Our Bible* (Chicago: Moody Press, 1974), ch. 7.
7. See Donald Guthrie, "The Canon of Scripture," *The New International Dictionary of the Christian Church* (Grand Rapids: Zondervan Publishing House, 1974), pp. 189, 190.
8. For a good discussion of the apocryphal books, see Norman L. Geisler and William E. Nix, *A General Introduction to the Bible.* (Chicago: Moody Press, 1976), pp. 162–207.
9. Alma 5:45, 46, *The Book of Mormon.* (Salt Lake City: The Church of Jesus Christ of Latter-Day Saints, 1950), p. 208.
10. *The Christian Science Journal* 3:7 (July, 1975) p. 362.
11. Ibid., p. 361.
12. *The First Church of Christ, Scientist and Miscellany* (Boston, 1941), p. 115.
13. *The Watchtower* (April 15, 1943) p. 127.
14. *Christianity Today* 21:10 (February 18, 1977) p. 18.

CHAPTER TEN

1. See William Hendriksen, *Exposition of the Gospel According to John,* Vol. 2. (Grand Rapids: Baker Book House, 1953), pp. 50–52.
2. For passages on God as Creator, see Genesis 1:1; Nehemiah 9:6; Job 26:7. For passages on God as Creator of man, see Genesis 1:26, 27; Job 12:10. For the eternity of God, see Job 36:26; Psalm 9:7; Ephesians 3:21; 1 Timothy 1:17. For God's faithfulness, see Psalms 100:5; 103:17; 121:3; 1 Corinthians 10:13; 2 Corinthians 1:20; 1 Thessalonians 5:24. For passages on the brevity of life, see 1 Samuel 23; Job 8:9; Psalm 90:9. For everlasting life, see John 5:24; 11:25; 1 John 2:25. For verses on death, see Romans 5:12; 1 Corinthians 15:21, 22; Hebrews 9:27.
3. For relationships between men and women and husbands and wives, see the Sermon on the Mount, Matthew 5–7; 1 Corinthians 7; Ephesians 5:21–33. For relationships between friends and enemies, see Proverbs 17:17; 27:10; 27:17; Matthew 5:43, 44; John 15:13.
4. For what the Bible teaches concerning what to eat and drink, see Romans 14:17–21; 1 Corinthians 10:31. For key passages on how to live, see Luke 6:31; Romans 12; Galatians 5:22–26. For verses on how to think, see Proverbs 12:5; Romans 12:3; Philippians 4:6–8.

CHAPTER ELEVEN

1. Alan Redpath, *Getting to Know the Will of God* (Downers Grove, Ill.: InterVarsity Press, 1954), p. 12.
2. Dwight L. Carlson, *Living God's Will* (Old Tappan, N. J.: Fleming H. Revell Company, 1976), pt. 3.
3. Jim Conway, *Men in Mid-Life Crisis* (Elgin, Ill.: David C. Cook Publishing Company, 1978). Chapters dealing particularly with sexual problems include chapters 10, 11, 15–19.
4. Barbara R. Fried, *The Middle-Age Crisis* (New York: Harper and Row Publishers, Inc., 1967), p. 39.
5. John F. MacArthur, Jr., *Found: God's Will* (Wheaton, Ill.: Victor Books, 1973).

CHAPTER THIRTEEN

1. Donald Guthrie, *The New Bible Commentary* (Grand Rapids: Wm. B. Eerdmans, 1970), p. 959.
2. William Barclay, *The Gospel of John* (Edinburgh: The Saint Andrew Press, 1955), pp. 172–176.
3. Some theologians have misconstrued the analogy of the vine and the branches to conclude that because the vinedresser, the Father, is a detached person who tends the vine, this proves that Christ was not a part of the Godhead. They argue that if Jesus' deity were genuine the Father would have been represented as something like the roots of the vine. But the point of Jesus' analogy is not to teach anything about His union with the Father. John has already stated quite conclusively that Jesus is God in several other places in his Gospel (see, for example, John 14:1–6). What Jesus is teaching here is the Father's care for the disciples of the Son.
4. For an excellent discussion of things that sometimes pass for fruit, see James E. Rosscup, *Abiding in Christ: Studies in John 15* (Grand Rapids: Zondervan Publishing House, 1973), pp. 70–77.
5. Question 1 of the Westminster Confession: "What is the chief end of man?" The answer: "Man's chief end is to glorify God and enjoy Him forever"—Westminster Assemblies Shorter Catechism.

CHAPTER FOURTEEN

1. For discussion of the Greek words *romphaia* and *machaira,* see W. E. Vine, *Expository Dictionary of New Testament Words* Vol. 4. (Old Tappan, N. J.: Fleming H. Revell Co., 1940), p. 100.
2. William Barclay, *The Gospel of Matthew* (Edinburgh: The Saint Andrew Press, 1956), p. 60.
3. A. Naismith, *1200 Notes, Quotes and Anecdotes* (Chicago: Moody Press, 1962), p. 15.

CHAPTER SIXTEEN

1. Charles R. Pfeiffer and Everett F. Harrison, eds., *The Wycliffe Bible Commentary* (Chicago: Moody Press, 1962), p. 62.
2. For more on a basic Bible reading plan, see Henry H. Halley, *Halley's Bible Handbook* (Grand Rapids: Zondervan Publishing House, 1965), pp. 805–813.
3. For information on the Navigator's Topical System, see Guidebooks One, Two, and Three. NavPress, P. O. Box 35001, Colorado Springs, Colorado 80901.

Index

P

R

S

Dr. John MacArthur, Jr., is the dynamic pastor and teacher of Grace Community Church in Sun Valley, California. His unwavering advocacy for a restoration of biblical theology in our time has won him the respect of both serious students of the Word and "people in the pews." His numerous books include *The Love of God, The Vanishing Conscience, Rediscovering Expository Preaching, Ashamed of the Gospel,* and *Our Sufficiency in Christ.* Dr. MacArthur is heard daily on the nationally syndicated radio broadcast, "Grace to You," which has sold more than ten million tapes.